No Sex Please . . .
We're Married

Gary Lautens

Illustrations by
Lynn Johnston

McClelland and Stewart

Second printing 1983

The articles in this book were first published
in *The Toronto Star* and *Canadian Star
Weekly* and appear with the kind
permission of the Toronto Star Syndicate.

McClelland and Stewart Limited
The Canadian Publishers
25 Hollinger Road
Toronto, Ontario
M4B 3G2

Canadian Cataloguing in Publication Data
Lautens, Gary.
   No sex please . . . we're married

A selection of the author's columns from the Toronto Star.
ISBN 0-7710-4723-1

1. Lautens family.   2. Family – Anecdotes, facetiae,
satire, etc.   I. Johnston, Lynn, 1947-   II. The
Toronto Star.   III. Title.

PN6231.F3L375   646.7'8'0207   C83-098809-2

Printed and bound in Canada
by T. H. Best Company Limited

Contents

Introduction

An introduction to a book is supposed to give the reader a taste of what is to follow so let me get to that bit of business immediately.

The articles here were written over a twenty-year period (from the early '60s to 1982) and concentrate on the main woman in my life, my co-vivant – dare I say it in this liberated age? – my wife. Her name is Jackie and I fell in love with her twenty-six years ago. Even better, we also fell deeply and meaningfully in like. As experts in the old man-woman thing know, like is very important if you want a relationship to last 125 or more years, which is my plan.

If I had to describe the one thing that makes me want to be home when the streetlights go on it's Jackie's sense of humour. In a phrase, she makes me laugh. And I hope she makes you laugh, too, because this book is mostly about the woman I refer to as the Resident Love Goddess.

Illustrations are by my friend Lynn Johnston, best known for her internationally acclaimed comic strip, For Better Or For Worse, but also illustrator of my last book, *Take My Family . . . Please!* Lynn managed the drawings while in the midst of planning a move with her dentist-husband and their children from Lynn Lake, Manitoba, to a new home in northern Ontario. No artist ever laboured under more trying conditions, and I appreciate it.

What else?

Oh, yes – the title.

When I started putting the material together, I asked my family for suggestions, always a dangerous approach if you know my family. My eldest (Stephen, who is now twenty-three) thought *Not Adolf Hitler's Diary* had commercial possibilities. Richard (who is eighteen) voted for *His and Herpes* just because he thought it had a nice ring. Daughter Jane (twenty-one) approved *Tee Hee For Two* and also leaned toward something a little naughty, *Oh, What A Lovely Pair!*, as a tribute to her mother and dad.

From the office came *Yes, We Have No Nirvanas* and *Everything's Coming Up Neuroses*. My wife's preference was *Love At First Laugh* or *The Party's Never Over*.

Finally, we settled for the title you see on the jacket – *No Sex Please . . . We're Married*. Even if you don't like it, I suggest it's better than Richard's second choice, *I Do, We Do – But No Dog Do*.

I should point out these stories appeared originally in the Panorama section of the defunct *Canadian Star Weekly* and in *The Toronto Star*. Some of the facts have been updated for 1983 but I've chosen to leave some stuff as written. Do not accuse me of being lazy. If you could be reported once more at ten years less your real age, wouldn't you leap at the chance, too? This is written, you see, by a happy man whose only regret is that it has all gone much too fast.

Gary Lautens

July, 1983

In the Beginning . . .

Why can't a woman remember like a man?

Usually I've got a pretty good memory. For example, I can remember my first car (a 1947 Ford), my first kiss (her name was Joan and it was 1945), my first job ($3 a week in 1941 for putting up baseball scores at the Hamilton *Spectator*).

Oh, yes, I can recall details from way back.

But I can't remember the first time I mentioned marriage to my wife. I don't remember proposing.

Let me explain right away that I don't drink or smoke pot, nor have I been struck on the head by a blunt object recently.

So that's not it.

I just don't remember. And, as a result, I have to depend on my wife to fill in the details about how I got married.

"Let's get this straight," I said to her the other night. "Explain to me how I wound up married."

"We've gone over this a hundred times," she replied. "Let's not do it again."

"Just once more," I begged. "For the record."

"Very well," she surrendered. "It was in 1956 . . ."

"I can remember 1956 perfectly," I said. "That was the year Edmonton beat Montreal for the third straight time in the Grey Cup. Jim Trimble was coaching the Hamilton Tiger-Cats and . . ."

"That's right," my wife interrupted. "The Tiger-Cats were running their contest to select Miss Tiger-Cat and you were one of the judges."

"So far, so good," I encouraged.

"You sat next to me at a luncheon — I was wearing a brown outfit with matching hat," my wife continued. "It was the twenty-first of October."

"I remember the contest," I said. "You and a girl named Garee Nash were tied for first place and I voted for Garee Nash to break the deadlock."

"That's right – she got the fur coat," my wife stated. "And I wound up with you as a consolation prize."

"You seem to have skipped something," I complained. "I don't remember running up to you and saying, 'Take me! I'm yours!'"

"Of course you didn't. You asked me out for dinner and a hockey game about a week later. You had a cream sports car and . . ."

"Get on to the part where I asked you to marry me," I suggested.

"You didn't ask me that night," my wife stated. "You asked me to marry you on our third date."

"Are you positive?" I asked.

"Don't you remember? We had been out to a movie. It was in November. And we were parked in your car in front of my place. You said . . ."

"Tell me exactly," I demanded.

"You said, 'If I had my way, there'd be something on that finger of yours.'"

"Maybe I meant gloves," I said. "After all, it was November and that was a cold car."

"Silly! You meant an engagement ring."

"Is that what I meant?"

"Of course."

"What did you say?"

"I was shocked," my wife recalled. "I told you we had only had three dates and it was nonsense to talk about marriage. Besides, I was only eighteen. You were twenty-eight."

"So I dropped the subject," I added.

"You wouldn't take 'no' for an answer," she contradicted. "I asked for time to think it over but you were too overpowering."

"I wish you'd explain that," I said.

"You sent flowers, candy, notes," my wife revealed. "Then, on December 2, you gave me a magnifying glass – and a diamond ring."

"What did you do?" I wanted to know.

"I didn't want to accept it. We hadn't known each other even two months."

"So you gave the ring back?"

"I wanted to," my wife informed me. "But I knew that would break your heart."

"Oh," I said.

"You set April 6 as our wedding date and said you couldn't live a moment longer without me," my wife concluded. "I didn't have a choice."

Anyway, that's the way it happened.

And, if you don't believe my wife, ask her mother.

Behind every successful man is a goof-off friend

Some people get ahead in this world through marriage and, although I'm not proud of the fact, I'm one of them.

In fact, marriage and promotion were virtually simultaneous in my particular case.

I know what you're thinking – that I married the boss's daughter or at least a very close niece.

But that wasn't how it was at all.

The girl I married worked as a secretary in a soap factory and the contacts she had were with Mr. Clean, not Roy Thomson or John Bassett.

Still, if I hadn't got married, I'd probably still be chasing ambulances and writing obituaries for ninety bucks a week.

Just for the record, let me explain what marriage did for my career in journalism.

I can remember getting up on my wedding day, throwing open the window to let in the morning sunshine, and thinking to myself, "Should I, or shouldn't I, jump?"

Like every other bridegroom, I felt that the idea I had six months before (the idea of getting married) didn't seem nearly so hot now that the actual day had arrived.

I made a mental note of all the drawbacks of getting married — the expense, the problem of getting into the bathroom for the rest of my life, the pain of having to give up my own room and Mom's cooking.

I then put down all the reasons why I should get married.

The best one I could think of was my wife-to-be's father. He is 6 feet 3, 220 pounds, a former football player, and a very poor loser. It seemed to me that I stood a very good chance of going through life with a fist sticking out the side of my face if I didn't go through with the marriage.

So I started to get dressed.

The wedding ceremony was scheduled for the early afternoon and it came off without a hitch except for the fact that my wife wore a silky dress and she kept slipping off the satin cushion when we knelt in front of the minister.

First she'd slide to the right, then to the left. Finally, she compromised by putting one knee on the cushion and anchoring the other on the floor. It gave her a 20-degree list to starboard but that didn't bother my wife. A girl doesn't have to be on the level to make it legal — as long as the guy says, "I do."

After the church service, we went downtown for the reception, where we had all the trimmings: a big cake, a lovely buffet, and a bunch of relatives glaring at each other, trying to figure out who got the best of the match.

It was a good party and still going strong when my bride and I finally left around six o'clock to start our car trip to Florida, where we spent our honeymoon.

Still confused?

Well, so was I when I got back from Florida and found I had a new title, new responsibilities, and a fatter pay cheque waiting for me at the office.

On the honeymoon, my wife promised she'd take me to the top. She pointed out that behind every successful man there's a woman – but frankly, I didn't expect such quick results. I thought I might have to wait a day or two before making my mark in the newspaper game.

But here I was, not back in the office fifteen minutes and already climbing toward the executive washroom.

Then I found out why.

Naturally, I had invited a lot of my friends to my wedding and the reception that followed.

One of them (as I discovered) had so much fun at the reception that he didn't go home for several days – or to the office.

To put it mildly, the office was furious.

Anyway, I got his job.

So now you know how I found fame and fortune through marriage.

It sure beats night school.

The funny things that happened after dark

It's been years since my wife and I moved into our first home – a two-bedroom bungalow in the suburbs that cost $11,500. And we only lived in that house a short time. But I'd still like to explain a few things to my old neighbours, wherever they are.

Like about the lights.

Our lights used to flick on and off at the strangest times. For example, the house might be in complete darkness by seven o'clock in the evening. On the other hand, every bulb in the entire place was often ablaze at three a.m.

That sort of thing can disturb any block and I wonder now what the people around us used to think. Did they figure we were running an all-night diner on the side? Did they suspect we were operating on European time? Or did they merely put us down as eager newlyweds who didn't rate sleep very high on our list of priorities?

I suspect the latter.

In any case, I want to put the record straight and tell the old neighbours just what was going on in the house they whispered about.

In the first place, I should explain that my wife and I practically went from the church to the bungalow with no stops in between.

Before we got married, I decided to sell my yellow sports car to scrape enough money for a down payment on a house. No apartment for us. I wanted to start off with a landlord that I like – me.

That was fine except for a couple of things. One was that

neither of us knew the first thing about how to run a house. Especially Jackie. For example, it wasn't unusual for my bride to plug half a dozen appliances into the same electrical circuit. That accounted for many of the blackouts our neighbours witnessed. The couple in No. 7 weren't hugging and kissing. They were downstairs in the basement, trying to find the damn fuse box.

Now for the second problem. Jackie had never been away from her parents before and moving into her own home was a strange experience.

To put it politely, Jackie was nervous. She kept hearing noises in the basement and seeing shadows in the yard. When I was around, that was no problem. We could hide under the bed together.

However, it just so happens that I worked a lot of nights at that time. Needless to say, it wasn't much of a life for a bride, especially one who was chicken about the dark. To put it bluntly, Jackie couldn't sleep a wink when I wasn't around to offer at least token protection.

Finally, she made her compromise. We'd go to bed right after she came home from work (Jackie was a secretary at the time) and get up around midnight. Jackie would pack me off to work – and then turn on every light in the place and do housework until dawn.

By the time I got home, the ironing would be finished, the washing would be finished, and Jackie would be finished, too. We'd both collapse in bed for a few hours of sleep and then start all over.

Fortunately, I didn't work every night in the week so sometimes we had normal hours.

But I can remember one neighbour who remarked he had seen me turn off the lights right after supper on the previous night.

"That's the fourth time this week," he commented.

Then he shook my hand, gave me a wink, and bet a dollar

that I'd be dead by the time I was thirty-five.

I hate to shoot down the reputation I falsely built up in those years.

But a buck's a buck.

Pledging undying love is a problem

I've got a problem. Our wedding anniversary is coming up and I don't know what to get my wife.

Years ago buying her a present was a snap. All I ever did was look around for some sexy line in Latin or French and then buy a piece of jewellery for it to be inscribed on.

In fact, that's how our romance got started. I got hold of this verse somewhere:

> Omnia vincit amor:
> et nos adamus amori.

Which, translated, means:

> Love conquers all:
> Let us, too, yield to love.

Well, I had that slapped on a silver makeup case before you could say "Rudolph Valentino."

Frankly, I felt guilty sending such high-powered stuff to an eighteen-year-old girl who, up till then, figured the height of romance was being allowed to carry her boyfriend's spikes home from a baseball game.

But I meant business.

The clincher, I think, was a photograph I sent to my wife-to-be that had this simple inscription:

Toujours et peut-être plus encore.

Yes – "Forever and, perhaps, a little longer."

After that it was just a matter of sticking around to cash in the chips. My Juliet didn't know what the hell I was talking about but she was curious enough to marry me to find out. Besides, she was tired of carrying around the baseball spikes.

That was twelve years ago. And that's the reason I've got the headache.

After twelve years of washing my socks and seeing me prance around the house in my corrective shorts, my wife isn't likely to be taken in again by any inscription, even if it's in Swahili.

My bachelor brother has a surefire gimmick. He sends unsuspecting young things a silver identification bracelet with only his telephone number engraved on the front. But if I pulled something like that on my wife now, she would probably fall over her vacuum cleaner in laughter.

So all my good stuff is out. I can't send her a doorknob (as I did in 1956) and claim I bit it off while waiting impatiently for our next date. The same goes for routine items like huge boxes of chocolates. (Chocolate makes her break out now.) And it's a little too soon to send her a nice cane with a rubber tip and her social security number scratched in the handle.

So here I am stuck in the middle years.

We've talked about going back to the motel where we spent our wedding night – a place called the Golden Gate – and trying to get room 5 again. But it's nearly ninety miles away. Besides, we don't like to leave the kids overnight and it wouldn't be quite the same if we took them with us.

We've thought about getting our wedding party together for a reunion. However, two of them are now divorced; another is a widow; and one of the bridesmaids is pretty pregnant. It doesn't have the makings of a swinging party.

Our TV cost $65 for repairs. I suppose that could always be considered our anniversary present. On the day itself – a Sunday – we could sit around, watch TV, maybe even send out for a pizza after the kids have gone to bed.

We could . . .

What's that jeweller's telephone number again?

Love letters: why don't women throw them out?

After years of marriage, a man is conditioned to face practically anything. He can survive rush hour traffic, a huge mortgage, Top Twenty records, income tax forms, and a kid who says, "Do I hafta?" But one thing still brings him to his knees – his old love letters.

For some strange reason, women never throw away a note written in passion. They adore heavy breathing, provided it comes in an envelope.

My wife, unfortunately, is no exception. Put an X at the bottom of a page of paper and my wife immediately wraps it in a blue ribbon and stashes it in her cedar chest. As a result, she has a bundle of old letters the size of a giraffe's goitre locked away.

And it's embarrassing.

Don't get me wrong. I plead guilty. I wrote all that stuff. Yes, I did say it was an eternity between kisses, that life is empty without her, and that I won't be satisfied until she's mine. I may even have commented on the sky being jealous of the blue in her eyes.

But does my wife have to remind me? If there's one thing a guy doesn't need, it's having a lot of nice things he wrote fifteen years ago thrown back in his face. Certainly I stated I wanted her in my arms. But that was in 1957, before the postal rates went sky-high. You could make a naughty suggestion then for a fraction of what it costs today. Besides, I was only a boy of twenty-eight at the time and didn't know what I was doing.

In any case, those old love letters are coming back to haunt me with a new generation. My daughter Jane (who is nine) has discovered where her mother keeps the literature from our courting days. And Jane would give both pigtails to get her hands on those letters for just fifteen minutes. She'd love to know what the old man had in mind when he was dating.

If she ever finds out, the old image will sure be shot to heck.

Suburbia

I just can't afford to become a celebrity

My wife's going to kick herself if I ever amount to anything — you know, win a Nobel prize for chemistry, write a terrific symphony, quarterback the Argos to a Grey Cup, that sort of thing.

Over the weekend we had a garage sale and Jackie sold my old desk for $20. It's thirty years old, and we can't take it to the new house (no room), so she felt it was a fair price.

But what if I become Prime Minister, or discover a cure for the common cold next week? Jackie will be furious she didn't ask at least $40 for the desk.

That's a chance you take when you hold a garage sale. You put price tags on the items, and then keep your fingers crossed that the original owner (in this case, me) isn't going to ruin everything by becoming famous.

Take our old bed. Provided I don't become the first person to go to Mars, or score 100 goals in a regular NHL season, the $15 we got for it is a fair price. After all, Jackie had the bed as a child; we slept in it the first few years of our marriage; and our eldest has used it the past ten years. So the doctor who bought it (for his summer cottage) was happy with the deal, and so were we.

However, I'll have to remain obscure to keep it that way. If I go into the movies and become another Fred Astaire, for example, I'll mess up everything.

In particular, I'm going to keep on my toes in the next few years and make sure I don't become the father of any country like George Washington. If I do, you can be sure the doctor who bought our bed will slap a brass plate on the headboard stating, "Gary Lautens, father of Ruritania, slept here," and charge $1 to see it.

If that dark day ever comes, my wife will be so mad at herself for letting a golden opportunity slip through her fingers, she might never speak to me again.

As I watched customers walk out of our garage with easy chairs, wine glasses, books, our picnic table, an old tow rope, garden furniture, pictures, and dozens of other items, I could feel the pressure mount.

Never in my life has failing been so important. Can you imagine what that stuff would be worth if The Who ask me to join their group, or I invent an engine that runs on pollution?

Fortunately, I've been able to avoid celebrity so far, but how long will my luck hold out? What if, by accident, I become a famous general, or get discovered by a Hollywood agent while sitting at the soda fountain in a local drugstore? What then?

I just hope my wife's lack of faith in me isn't unjustified.

Passing the trash test

There are moments in life when you put your reputation on the line: risk prestige, image, and good name on one toss of the dice. Trash day in the suburbs is one such moment.

Twice a year you're allowed to put out junk at the curb and have it collected, free of charge, by the city or town. Mattresses, ancient ice boxes, wheelless tricycles – they're all eligible for pick-up.

However, before your discards vanish they're judged by

your neighbours. On trash night, every one is out, cruising up and down the streets to see what's up for grabs, and assessing the quality of your throwaways.

Naturally we try to keep up, but it isn't always easy to find something good enough to put out in broad daylight. The best we could come up with this year was a pair of kitchen chairs that have been down in the basement for a couple of years, an old golf cart (but still in working order), a bamboo pole, an empty barrel used for pool chemicals, and a push broom with some bristle showing.

Frankly, it didn't compare with the best trash on the street. I think Gards won that honour with a toboggan that looked almost brand new, or it could have been the new people who put out a fold-up bed.

Still, I thought our junk was a good average and could hold its own with most of the stuff stacked on the street. At least we didn't have boring chunks of concrete, or a tacky tire covered with blow-out patches. However, until somebody drives up and picks up your son's old wagon or the deck chair with no seat, you never know if your trash really measures up.

Nothing is more embarrassing than putting out your trash on trash night, and having it still intact next morning when the official pick-up takes place. It means you've really struck out, that not even the neighbourhood kids (who'll pick up anything) want your rubbish.

My wife stood nervously by the front window to see how long it would take for some one to pick through our stuff; she was certain the golf cart would be snapped up first.

Well, she was wrong. The bamboo pole was grabbed about thirty minutes after our curb opened for business, and the cart followed that, and then the kitchen chairs (which were badly ripped and not a hot item, in my estimation).

By morning, when the official pick-up trucks arrived, all we had left at the front of our place was a pail of odds and ends, and my wife never expected them to move.

So she was delighted.

Even better, I gave our kids strict orders not to bring home anybody else's trash because we're in the process of moving and don't need more clutter. Except for a large paper rose, an umbrella that practically works, and part of a skateboard, they followed my instructions to the letter.

These trash days sure are hard on the nerves.

The joys of being alone

At this very moment I'm trying to write a column at home. The kids are at school; my wife is at her exercise class at the Y; and the dog is outside in the yard.

Yes, I'm alone.

Perfect, you say?

Wrong. The racket in the house is driving me up the wall.

Brrr-ummm. Click, click, click, click. Klackety-klack. Chug-a-boom, chug-a-boom. Ker-bang, ker-bang.

My ears are ready to fall off.

The reason, of course, is that I am the twentieth-century man and home is not a home; it's a hydro sub-station. Sure, my wife is at the Y, running her little heart out, doing push-ups, and taking a dip in the pool to maintain her body tone. But the housework goes on whether or not she's on the premises.

This, for example, is Monday, and Monday is washday. So, before my wife packed her sweatsocks into her gym bag, she packed everybody else's socks (and other dainties) into the automatic washer. She also loaded the breakfast dishes into the automatic dishwasher. She dumped a few damp things (including a pair of Richard's running shoes) into the automatic dryer. She put lunch into the automatic oven. She set the thermostat on the automatic furnace to click on at 75. (My wife hates to come home to a cold house after working out all morning over a hot barbell.) She checked the automatic humidifier. She adjusted the automatic timer on the radio so she wouldn't miss Gordon Sinclair.

And then she activated the entire system before ducking out of the electronic jungle we call home.

So here I am, sitting in the midst of whirring gears, squirting hoses, and an assortment of switches flicking on and off with no help from me.

The only thing that isn't automated is the typewriter – and I'm supposed to make it work. But how can I concentrate with all this cleaning, washing, etc. going on?

Do they manufacture a transistor that can be implanted in a columnist's nose (or spleen), something the lady of the house can set for 500 words when she's throwing the toggle switch on her other labour-saving devices? I hope so because getting anything done when you're alone in the house nowadays is impossible.

I sure miss the kids, the dog, and my wife. At least when they're around, they keep it down to a low roar.

On middle-aged antiques

Whenever my wife gets her hands on a few bucks these days

she rushes out to buy something old for the house. Yes, she's on an antique kick.

Maybe "old" is the wrong word. We can't afford old. The stuff we get is more middle-aged, old enough to vote but not quite old enough to have hardening of the drawers.

This past weekend, for example, she picked up a wash stand at a flea market back in the country. The price on the tag was $150 but my wife, coming from thrifty English stock, WASPed the dealer down to $110.

According to my wife, it's the very thing she's been looking for to fill in the blank spot in the living room. It has everything – wobbly legs, a stone counter top with a big chip in it, lots of stains on the wood, and a missing door handle.

Of course, my wife would have preferred a wash stand with two missing door handles – but that would have been out of our price range.

"Isn't it gorgeous?" my wife asked when she first spotted the treasure. "Don't you just love those old blue tiles across the top of the wash stand?"

I told her "love" was probably too strong a word. "Like" would be closer; "hate" would be dead-on.

Naturally she wasn't listening. She closed the transaction and gave me instructions to load her purchase into the car.

As any one who goes to country flea markets, auctions, or swap shops knows, there is one irrefutable law: whatever your wife buys, it will always be long enough, wide enough, or deep enough to make it impossible to close the trunk of your car. It is also heavy enough to make the veins stand out on your forehead and give you a stabbing pain in the groin.

Anyway, trunk open, kids fighting, wash stand loaded, we zoomed home along the highway at a steady ten miles an hour – "make sure you don't scratch it," my wife cautioned. In the antique game, they only want old scratches, not new ones.

So now the wash stand is in our living room, a mere 2,569 man-hours of sanding, staining, and cursing away from being a gleaming jewel among our possessions.

But I shouldn't complain. If my wife didn't have this weakness for middle-aged, beat-up stuff with wobbly legs, where would I be today?

Rosebuds, pressed flowers, and a flooded basement

During the coldest night of the winter, a water pipe burst in our home and flooded the entire downstairs area – the family room, a playroom, the spare bedroom, and my office. Rugs were ruined, including broadloom put down only a week earlier; floors heaved; the ceiling drooped at a dangerous angle; the TV was doused.

Even worse, Jackie lost her rosebuds.

That may not seem tragic to you but my wife's rosebuds have always been important to her. I must admit, I've grown attached to them too, over the years.

They were taken from our wedding cake, carefully wrapped in plastic, then stored with our other valuables under the front stairs. Because they were sugar rosebuds, we didn't take them out often – but it gave us a warm feeling to know they were there if we wanted them.

So you can imagine the panic on the morning of the flood when Jackie saw the water pouring out of the ceiling and swirling in deep pools on the floor. Ignoring the floating furniture, Jackie wanted to dive immediately for her treasures.

Fortunately, a cool head prevailed. "Turn off the water first," I ordered, handing her a pair of rubber boots. "Then we'll see if we can save your rosebuds."

As it turned out, we were too late. Jackie's rosebuds were goners by the time the water was stopped and pumped out of the house by a crew of men (for a big fee, incidentally).

Picking through the damp rooms after the workmen were packed and leaving, Jackie came up with a soggy cardboard container. Yes – the carton where all the souvenirs of our honeymoon had been stored. The sugar rosebuds were just puddles of coloured water.

"Our wedding invitations are ruined too," Jackie groaned. "Look."

What she held up looked like a clumsy U-boat commander's lunch.

According to Jackie our total loss was (1) four rosebuds, (2) a half dozen leftover invitations inviting the receiver to the wedding reception of Jaqueline Joan Lane and Gary Lautens on April 6, 1957, and (3) the pressed flowers from her wedding bouquet.

The loss of the floor, ceiling, and broadloom was strictly incidental.

Happily, Jackie was able to salvage some of her souvenirs. For example, the blue garter she wore on her wedding day survived with plenty of snap. So did a blue hanky that was part of the wedding bouquet.

And, after working on them with a warm iron, my wife was able to present me with some other remembrances of the honeymoon trip.

To wit: a receipt for $6 for room 5 at the Golden Gate Motel (I was nervous when I signed the register and got my address wrong.); a written warning from a Florida state trooper for doing 70 mph in a 60 mph zone (It was difficult enough explaining to my mother why it took us six days to cover 1,600 miles without having to explain a speeding ticket, too.); a menu from Hollywood, Florida (Full course meals, $1.45 up.); and, finally, a postcard of the apartment-motel where we stayed by the ocean in Florida ($70 per week), plus a business card from the Polka Dot Gift Shoppe, souvenirs a specialty.

It's going to cost plenty to get everything straightened around at the house but Jackie has only one question on her mind: how come we didn't have rosebud insurance?

Bargain at the cleaners

Don't invite us over for the next couple of days. We can't come. My wife doesn't have a thing to wear. And I'll tell you how it happened.

Yesterday, Jackie decided to take a pair of slacks to the cleaners. And, while she was there, she spotted a sign pasted on the wall.

It said: "Today's special! Any red article of clothing dry-cleaned free with a $3 regular order. Jackie's eyes lit up. "Is that any red article?" she asked the clerk in the cleaning shop.

"That's what the sign says," was the response.

"What time do you close?"

"In about twenty minutes," the clerk said.

"Is the special on again tomorrow?"

"No."

Jackie was in a dilemma. There wasn't time to go home and fetch something – anything – red. But the bargain! That's when the light went on.

My wife realized she did have something red with her – her overcoat. She started to take it off. The other customers gawked.

"What are you doing?" a slightly shocked clerk wanted to know.

"You said you'd take any red article of clothing, didn't you?" Jackie replied.

"Well, yes – but it's zero outside. How are you going to get home without a coat?"

"I'll manage," my wife said.

She emptied the pockets of her red overcoat, picked up her cleaning ticket – and walked out into the blizzard.

That's how she came home – coatless.

"I've just saved $6.50," she announced proudly, shivering in the front hall. Then she explained what had happened.

Thank God the cleaners didn't have a special on articles of clothing in pink with little daisies on the top. I hate to imagine how Jackie would have come home.

The egg man cometh

Somebody's come between my wife and me. It's our egg man. Every Monday morning my wife leaves me in charge of the house while she trots off to her exercise class. And every Monday morning her last instructions are: "Don't get any eggs today."

Thirty minutes later there's a knock on the door. Yes – the

egg man. And I buy another tray of eggs. To put it bluntly, I can't say no to the egg man.

Oh, I can get up on my typewriter and lecture the PM, the president, or even the pope. I'm not reluctant to tell General Motors where to get off. But the egg man is another matter.

Believe me, I try to be firm. I practise saying, "No eggs today, thank you." However, my refusals vanish when I come face to face with my Monday morning visitor. He raps on the back door, comments on the weather, smiles – and the next thing I know I've got another three dozen grade A large on my hands.

Maybe it's the way he pulls his tweed cap down over his ears. Maybe it's the way he talks to our dog. Or maybe he's an amateur hypnotist. All I know is I'm putty in his change purse.

Unfortunately, my wife doesn't understand. Women seldom do, especially those with a refrigerator already bulging with eggs. For one thing, my wife never fails to point out, nobody in our family likes eggs. Except me. To take off some of the heat, I eat eggs as often as I can; but ten to fifteen a week is my limit. Any more than that and I get a curious urge to climb up on the roof at dawn and cock-a-doodle-doo at anything passing in feathers.

Because I can't keep up with the supply, after a few weeks we usually have enough eggs on hand to stage a student riot – unless I can palm off a couple of dozen on mother.

What's the answer?

My wife has threatened to pin a sign to my shirt which reads: "Do not sell eggs to this husband." Or else we could move and hope the egg man never finds me.

Shopping holiday for stay-at-homes

Nobody's going to be more sorry to see the summer end than the Lautens family. For the last couple of months we've been living on something even better than borrowed time. We've been getting along on borrowed groceries. That's the advantage of living on a block where everybody goes away on holidays.

As our neighbours pack up to leave for the cottage or on a car trip, they invariably find something in the refrigerator they can't take with them. It can be anything from half a quart of milk to a chocolate pie with only one piece missing – but rather than throw it out, they want to give it to somebody.

And that's where we come in. We're the "somebody" who stays home in July and August and picks up the district's delicious discards.

For example, just last evening there was a knock on the door about 11 o'clock.

Marion (who lives next door) apologized for disturbing us so late but said she was leaving in the morning and could we use some butter, a loaf of bread, and half a watermelon she had in her refrigerator. We said we'd be glad to take them off her hands. They'll go nicely with the almost-full bottle of ginger ale, the rice pudding, and the fruit tarts we got from Isobel earlier this week.

And I can't wait for Sam and Pat to go on their trip. Pat's usually good for at least one berry pie and her crust is as good as anyone's on the block.

Food isn't the only dividend to stay-at-homes. My neighbour Ed has been working like a slave all year in his garden but he's going to be away for most of this month. So he told me to help myself to his tomatoes, beans, and raspberries. Which I've been doing.

I haven't planted anything more spectacular than myself (and only in the hammock out in the backyard) but I've got all the fresh fruit and vegetables I can handle. Thanks to good old Ed, we've even got flowers on the dinner table these nights. He sure plants a mean daisy.

I enjoyed Ron's football tickets (he's in Florida) and Harold's lawn chairs (he's down east) and Mark's barbecue (he's up north). If I want, there's Clarke's pool and Jim's second car, not to mention every magazine published in the English-speaking world. (We take in the neighbour's mail, natch.)

Frankly, when you consider the high cost of living, I'm amazed that people go anywhere in the summer.

My wife doesn't "work"

Is there anything more embarrassing today than being married to a woman who doesn't "work"?

Take Jackie.

She weaves, spins wool, attends classes twice a week at the Ontario College of Art, and is currently putting together a seven-foot tapestry she designed for the living-room. She also whips up 100 meals a week, irons a dozen shirts, waxes and washes the floors, walks the dog, throws a dinner party once a week.

But she doesn't "work."

She feels a minimum of two foreheads a week (to see if they're warm), listens to enough homework to get a degree from Oxford, runs the family budget, finds things in the basement no other living human being can find, reminds Richard to comb his hair every morning, cheers up Jane when she gets a zit on her face, and refinishes furniture.

She does the shopping, locates the bargains, washes gym stuff, keeps track of everybody's underwear, answers family mail, makes certain nobody leaves a ring around the bathtub, takes care of minor medical problems.

But she doesn't "work."

She cuts hair, cleans the filter on the furnace, clips the dog's nails, provides waltz lessons for male members of the family, vacuums, puts treats in school lunchbags for a noonday surprise, hangs up coats, holds feet when they get cold, provides laughs when needed or not, removes splinters, gives instruction on the application of eyeshadow, announces if it's a boot day, smiles through the recounting of old Monty Python skits, files class photographs.

She doesn't let anyone out of the house without a hug; she tucks Jane into bed every night (even though Jane is fourteen and almost as big as her mother); she knows the postal rates, moves chesterfields, listens solemnly when someone in the house says he or she is going to be prime minister, a famous athlete, or just an astonishing detective (Richard's current ambition); she hangs pictures (eighty on our one wall), sews on buttons, visits art galleries.

But "work"? I'm afraid not.

Jackie lengthens jeans, unplugs plumbing, remembers to serve spaghetti once a week (the kids' favourite), picks out newspaper items that might make columns, does thirty situps every morning to stay trim, explains patiently to Richard why he can't wear the same shirt eighteen days in a row, and makes the Christmas cards.

Mind you, she doesn't jog three times a week now, act as lifeguard at the "Y," or take German at night school, and her university class on great books is over.

But she did broadloom Jane's bedroom, make our front room coffee table (from an old dining-room suite), and (just last week) figure out how to replace the bulb in our slide projector when Daddy had failed.

That is, unfortunately, beside the point.

Jackie does not go to an office, perform brain surgery under OHIP, drive a truck, belong to a union, type up letters, sell real estate, host a TV show, or wrestle at Maple Leaf Gardens.

In short, she doesn't "work."

Mind you, she did "work" the first three years we were married and trying to get a start, but she quit a month or two before she had Stephen.

So she's just a homemaker, wife, and mother now.

Perhaps one day when the kids are a little more grown up, Jackie will "work" again, but in the meantime, I'm afraid she's too busy.

Living next to a work nut

As everybody knows, a man wants only one thing out of life – a neighbour who is lazier than himself. That's human nature.

Unfortunately, I live next door to the work champion of the entire world. This guy has every fault in the book – ambition, energy, industry, and a complete set of tools, which never leaves his hands.

He is a sweat nut and I hate him.

Compared to my neighbour, Pierre Berton is a drifter. Every

weekend I just get propped up in a soft chair when my wife says: "Ed's out raking the leaves." Or, "Ed's rebuilding his sundeck." Or, "Ed's bringing in his corn." Or some other darn thing.

Ed never sits down. His lawn is the first one cut. He catches snowflakes in mid-air before they even land on his driveway. His garage is neat as a pin and his windows (front and back) just sparkle, for heaven's sake. It's enough to make you sick.

Naturally, with that kind of competition, I'm forced to do all sorts of things that I'd ordinarily let slip.

To make things worse, Ed is a "helper." When he sees a tree in my yard that looks sick, he brings over a saw and suggests we cut it down together. He's been after me to put up a sundial I was given barely two years ago. "I'll bet we could do it in a weekend," Ed has told me at least a hundred times. "A little digging, some cement . . ." Most people have consciences; I have Ed.

He ran me ragged all summer but Ed really went too far about a week ago. I was just home from work when my wife said: "Ed's painting his house."

Ed's house was painted only two years ago but, sure enough, he was at it again. And he didn't even have his wife helping him. That's what I call flaunting it.

All evening I seethed. How can a man sprawl on the chesterfield, kick off his shoes, and enjoy himself, knowing that sort of thing is going on next door?

Ed waved and shouted to me that he had mixed up a special water resistant stain for his wooden siding and expected to finish the house in a couple of days. He said we could start my place next. I just smiled – weakly.

Ed wasn't on his ladder the following day and I noticed his special stain hadn't dried. In fact, it was still wet yesterday when a professional painter came over and gave Ed a price on how much it would cost to sand down the house and re-do the job.

Last night I saw Ed inside his house watching TV. It's the

first night off Ed has given us in three years and every husband on the block is delighted.

I just hope it lasts.

The writing on the wall

Few groups in society are sadder than those people who go around printing dirty words on walls – except, of course, the even more unfortunate souls who try to erase the dirty words the other group has scribbled.

The other morning I was walking the dog before breakfast when my neighbour Len pulled to the curb. "I hate to be the bearer of bad news," he said, "but somebody's written THAT word in letters two feet high on the side of your house. And it's on the brick."

Yes, between dusk and dawn, someone with a paint bomb had sprayed THAT word on the side of our house.

Of course, when I saw it, my first thought was about the author. Did he or she have an unhappy childhood? Is this his or her way of crying out for attention? Was society really to blame?

My second thought was how to get the graffiti removed before being raided by the morality squad for keeping an obscene wall.

Alas, while thousands of dollars have been spent on delving into the minds of people who express themselves by jotting down naughty things in places where they can be seen, not a dime (as far as I can learn) has been directed to research programs aimed at removing their handiwork from walls, especially those made of rough brick. In fact, the first hardware store operator I called told me flatly, "It will never come off. I'd advise you to move."

"On rough brick?" a good friend answered. "Why don't you add a couple of letters and make it into a nice word, or disguise it in a floral design?"

Unfortunately, although a graduate of a couple of educational institutions, I cannot for the life of me think of a word containing THAT word, at least none that's perfectly respectable. So that idea was discarded, too.

A chemical firm representative said acid might turn the trick. "But it might just clean up the brick and make the letters stand out even more," I was informed.

At that point I was prepared to paint a message under the one left by my mysterious caller, something like: "The preceding is a paid announcement and does not necessarily represent the opinion of this home-owner," and leave it at that.

Then I realized there was one expert on the subject of rude word removal – the janitor at the corner school.

I was right. In his years of obliterating coarse words from walls (so he informed me) he had enjoyed his best success with a product – here he named it – that didn't totally remove the bad phrases but did fade them to the extent they no longer caused a lot of giggling among the children.

Well, I tried it, and after three applications THAT word has almost disappeared. And it only cost $2, or fifty cents a letter.

Which leaves me with one thought for the day: our forefathers knew what they were doing when they decided to keep obscenities short.

Some dirty tricks are too much like work

Our neighbour Bev gives her husband Barry the same present every spring – a load of topsoil. It's amazing how many wives in suburbia do the very same thing. Why any husband would want a huge load of dirt, I don't know, and Barry isn't much help, either.

As soon as the dump truck unloaded its cargo Saturday morning (in Barry's driveway, of course) Barry came outside and walked around the dirt.

"What are you going to do with that?" I asked.

Barry smiled sheepishly, shrugged his shoulders, and didn't have any answer.

"Is that your Father's Day present?" shouted Jim from his yard next door.

Barry's smile was definitely weak as he circled the dirt, piled high enough to challenge all but an expert mountain-climber. Hands in his pockets, he stared at the topsoil, turned over a clump or two with his foot, and then disappeared into his house.

An hour or so later Barry and his wife came out of their house, got into the car, and carefully backed out around the dirt, a very difficult bit of manoeuvring.

They had just driven down the street when my wife came up with a terrific idea. "Wouldn't it be funny if you moved the topsoil while Barry's out?" she said. "Imagine the look on his face if he came home and found a ton of dirt gone from his driveway."

I broke out in laughter. "I can hear Barry now when he telephones the police. 'I'd like to report a load of topsoil missing. That's right – topsoil. It's brown and, when last seen, was about seven feet high, weighs around 2,000 pounds, and has no distinguishing marks or scars.' It would be a riot."

"I bet Jim would go along with you," my wife suggested. "All you'd have to get is a couple of wheelbarrows and shovels. If you start now, you could probably move the entire load before Barry and Bev get back from shopping."

"It would be a great practical joke," I agreed, slapping my knee and giggling so hard the tears began rolling down my cheeks. "With brooms we could sweep up the driveway so Barry wouldn't find even a trace of the dirt. He'd wonder if he had been dreaming."

My wife said we didn't have a moment to lose if we wanted to pull this fantastic gag on Barry.

However, I began figuring out how many shovelfuls of dirt were involved, how many trips (approximately) I'd have to make with the wheelbarrow, the problem I might have finding a place to bury a ton of dirt without Barry spotting it, and if it might bother my back which, up to now, has never given me any problems. It was with great reluctance that I finally abandoned the entire idea.

But next year when Barry gets his annual spring load of topsoil, I fully intend to do it.

Provided it's a nice day, of course, and I can find a shovel.

$100,000 fireplace – just grate

When we were looking for a house, my wife made only two stipulations: it had to be more than we could afford and it had to have a fireplace.

The first condition was no problem. Every place we looked at met that requirement, with thousands to spare. But the fireplace was another matter.

My wife wanted a big fireplace. Stone. Floor-to-ceiling. Something that would dominate the room and still have charm.

My wife didn't care if the house was made of brick, boards, or corn flakes. The basement was incidental. And the roof could have more leaks than a 29-cent pen.

When my wife stepped into a house, she immediately went to the fireplace. She looked up the chimney. She checked the firewall. She examined the mortar. She asked questions about the draught. And then she'd lean against the fireplace to see if it clashed with her hairstyle.

Finally, she found exactly what she was looking for – a dramatic, cosy fireplace with enough rooms attached to take care of the kids and make meals. Even better, thanks to the easy monthly payments, it could all be mine, provided I live to 186 and walk to work.

Naturally, with an opportunity like that, I snapped it up. I could see us living like a page out of *Home Beautiful* – midnight suppers around crackling logs, shadows dancing on the ceiling, filmy peignoirs, passionate glances shared over the kindling.

I should have my imagination checked because that's not how it's worked at all. The only thing dancing out at me at midnight is garbage. My wife stuffs everything in that fireplace – cake boxes, milk cartons, apple cores, leftover cloth, string, socks too tattered to mend, broken toys.

I live in the only $100,000 incinerator in town.

When my wife cleans up after supper, she has a theory: if it won't fit in the dog, it will fit in the fireplace.

I don't know if wood will burn in the fireplace. We've never tried it. But newspapers make a nice flame. Orange peels aren't bad. And the wrapping the bacon comes in is really hot stuff.

Naturally, there are advantages to my wife's trash program.

The children, for example, love to see the pretty glow of hot tin cans on a cold night and they think the smell of cooking banana peels is dreamy.

You must come around some night and see our pyre drill.

I give you one word of caution, though. Don't fall asleep in our family room – not unless you're too big to fit in the fireplace.

My wife is a bug for neatness.

Must the car of my dreams die?

According to the newspaper, it would take $4.5 million to save the mighty MG from being phased out this year and going the sad way of the Studebaker, Edsel, and Hudson Hornet.

Alas, a quick check of my own cash flow indicates I am $4,499,987.50 short of the fiscal mark, the holiday having left only $12.50 in my trouser pockets.

Too bad.

If I had the necessary folding stuff, I'd be off like a shot to the troubled British Leyland plant in southern England where the most respected of sports cars is made.

"Here's your piddling $4.5 million," I'd say, dumping the bank notes on a desk top with ill-concealed disdain. "That's a small price to pay for a treasured dream."

Yes, that would be the strategy if I wasn't a little short myself 'til payday.

My first car was an MG – a TF model in racing ivory with wire wheels, red leather upholstery, a 1250 cc engine, plastic side curtains, and a top speed of just over 80 mph. It cost me $2,400 in 1954 and was brand, spanking new.

On summer days I'd flop the windscreen flat, take off my shoes (the foot pedals were a little too close to be operated with size 11½ shoes), and seek out remote country roads where I could let her out and practise my "drifts" around sharpish corners.

Oh, what enchantment that was, little nuts and bolts shaking out of the dash at unexpected moments, the accelerator chattering at the idle under stockinged feet, a top that could be put up in the event of an unexpected cloudburst in less than fifteen minutes, provided you had help.

And then there was the heater.

The MG of that era was for purists and, of course, came without soul-softening frills like defroster or heater. However, I weakened when it became difficult to see the road through puffs of January breath.

A makeshift heater used in ambulances was installed in the cramped cockpit and, except for falling off at regular intervals, it worked fine. Better it should fall off than a vital part of my anatomy was my philosophy.

How I smirked at fake sports cars like the Thunderbird or Corvette when I tooled around town in my MG. How I lorded it over those who had springs in their cars and trunks for luggage.

For heaven's sake, the MG I drove had hardwood in its frame.

And the only mechanic I'd allow near it was a Brit named Harry Shute, a very tweedy type who always had a scarf around his throat and employed a stethoscope when listening for engine noises.

By George, those were the days. We MG drivers waved to each other on the road, many with gloved hands (although I never went quite that far). And we talked about mysterious things like RPMs, then quite unknown to owners of North American machinery.

Once a man (whose identity I won't disclose) put a garbage can on top of my MG as a gag, causing the canvas roof to droop down like a beige goitre. I would never have forgiven him but I wanted to marry his daughter.

Which brings up Jackie.

I would be driving that MG yet, I suppose, polishing the chrome, doing my own lube work and waxing the bonnet 'til I had houseperson's knee, but it was my only asset when I popped the question, the one about marriage, I mean.

So, at the risk of breaking your heart, I must reveal I sold the car for a down payment on a love nest, love nests going for $11,500 in those days. That was 1957.

Over the years I thought I might get another MG one day but the closest I've come is a Dinky toy model Jackie included in a Christmas present a few years ago.

Now, unless I find $4,999,987.50 on the street on the way home tonight, the dream of owning an MG will be over for a lot of us.

However, as my mother-in-law likes to sympathize, "by the time a man can afford a sports car, he doesn't look good in it anyway."

Mooning about our city

Those of us who live in the inner city get nostalgic, too, when summer ends. Of course we don't get mellow necessarily over flights of birds heading south, trees showing signs of scarlet, tiny animals scurrying to lay in supplies for cruel months ahead.

No, it isn't quite like that.

But we do have our special moments, moments that cause us to pause and reflect over the dying season.

Such a tender moment occurred the other day as Mrs. Lautens and I were drinking in sights we somehow instinctively know will soon fade from the inner city.

We were on Church St., only a few steps from Bloor, when it happened.

There were four young people ahead of us, two men, two women, and it was early evening, the sun not having disappeared yet in the sky behind the Asquith library.

Without any advance warning, one of the men dropped his trousers, exposing his bare behind.

It was only for a second, just a flash, and then the couples, laughing and giggling, continued on their way.

"I wouldn't be surprised if that's the last moon of summer," my wife reflected.

"You're probably right," I agreed sombrely.

Several years ago I wrote about the first moon of spring, an event witnessed near the same corner when somebody stuck unclad buttocks out the rear window of a passing car.

While the first moon of spring is a harbinger of the season ahead, and a happy event, there is something poignant about the last one of the season.

In not many weeks the autumn wind will have bite to it, making it dangerous for anyone to expose his or her bottom from a sedan window, on the street, or in a passing truck carrying engineering students to an initiation rite.

When the frost is on the pumpkin, nobody in his right mind wants to take a chance of getting frost on his personal pumpkin.

The stark truth is – mooning is finished for another year, unless we have an Indian summer or something.

"I wonder how long it will be before we see our next moon," Mrs. Lautens asked wistfully after our encounter. "Probably months."

In a philosophical vein I suggested the last moon of the season, like the last rose of summer, makes a person aware of the passing of time.

"It seems as if you spot your first moon of the year and, before you know it, you've seen your last," was the way I put it.

"Yes." Jackie said. "But Canadians probably appreciate mooning more than people who live in a warm climate where there is mooning year 'round."

I nodded, and both of us walked in silence for the next few blocks, thinking of the changing Canadian seasons, the end of summer, and (probably) the last moon of the year.

Downtown people are very sensitive, you know.

Song of Myself

98-pound weaklings — look out!

I go to the gym three times a week but I suppose you've already guessed. Fabulous bodies like mine don't just happen. They require a lot of work.

Of course having these enormous muscles isn't all fun. They are responsibilities, too. You have to go to the beach every Sunday and kick sand in the face of 98-pound weaklings and steal their girl friends. You have to leap tall buildings with a single bound (I find the tighter the leotards, the better the distance on those leaps). And you have to put up with people who confuse you for a movie star in one of those secret agent, bang-bang, action films that the English turn out. (Three times this week I was mistaken for Inspector Clouseau and twice for Elsa Lanchester.)

All this can be yours if you will only follow the proper workout schedule. The best way to start a workout is with a laugh, which explains the locker room where men take off their clothes. A man wearing only a double-breasted grin can't take himself too seriously and he immediately forgets his troubles at the office. He becomes a boy

Put him in a pair of shorts and some sneakers and he will do all sorts of silly things. Which brings up running. At our gym the instructor believes in running. He talks about it by the hour. He feels everybody should run a mile or two a day, even if he doesn't have a secretary.

All you need for running is two clever feet and one dumb head, he explains as he blows his whistle and lets us loose like a pair of whippets. Then he goes back in his office and reads magazines. Every now and then he comes out and checks our mileage by the distance our tongues are hanging down our chests. Unless you have a good excuse, like dropping dead, he expects you to run until your tongue falls over the laces of your tennis shoes.

As the survivors straggle in, he looks them over and states in a loud voice (it has to be loud to be heard over the thumping of hearts) that he just wishes the Russians could see us. "They don't realize what they're up against," he shouts.

We just lie there, remarking to each other how much he looks like Adolph Hitler and wondering if he'd accept a plane ticket to Argentina on his birthday.

Then we do some push-ups, clutching desperately to the floor so that we don't fall off. Sometimes we throw our legs over our heads (beginners get two throws) and touch our noses in all sorts of awkward places.

The hilarity lasts about forty-five minutes.

Some of us tried to get an insurance machine, like the ones at the airport, installed at the entrance of the gymnasium, the idea being that you could put in a quarter and be insured for the duration of the workout. But no company will touch it. They said they'd want to give us mental examinations before they'd even talk about insurance.

Anyway, we keep it up, three noons a week, running nowhere, filling the air with feet, bottoms, and profanity. Of course we can't do any other physical activity since we are always resting for the next workout. Besides, I have this sore knee now.

But it's worth it. The instructor said the workouts would make us live longer and it seems that way already. Some days are unbelievably long. He also says it will improve my wind. Right now, he claims, he would be willing to bet that nobody in Toronto has more wind than me.

Yes. Step a little closer. I could be persuaded to let you feel my muscle. It just came back from the dry cleaners.

Keeping fit

I've never felt better in my life, thanks to fitness classes. Three times a week I go to the gym. I run; I do push-ups; I play volleyball.

There's only one problem with being fit: I think my marriage is falling apart. You see, my wife can't keep up with me any more. I first noticed her slowing down a few months ago in the supermarket. She was pushing a grocery cart, holding the baby, and chasing the two other kids around the toilet paper displays.

"You're puffing," I told her at the time.

She admitted she was and asked if I'd mind holding the baby for a while.

I told her I'd love to. But I couldn't.

"I've got to go to the gym today," I reminded her. "Fitness classes don't do you any good unless you're fresh and relaxed."

"I'm sorry," she said. "I forgot."

I suppose the same thing happens a hundred times a week. My wife will be scrubbing the floor or putting up a bookcase or moving the chesterfield and she'll ask me to give her a hand.

"And risk pulling a muscle in my back!" I answer. "I've got a volleyball game today and it may mean a spot in the playoffs for the team."

So my wife does it herself.

Sometimes she asks me to carry something heavy into the basement after I've been to the gym. Of course I'm too tired by then. Besides, you're just asking for trouble if you exert yourself after a stiff workout. A sore back could put my training program back a week or ten days.

Right now I'm resting because I have to be at the gym in

five hours. My hand's steady. No circles under the eyes. Biceps perfectly relaxed.

But you should see my wife! I'd call her but she's outside shovelling snow. Her hands are red and rough. She has a stiff neck from trying to lift the washer. And lines are creeping into her face. It will take her three hours to clear out a driveway that should be done in two, two-and-a-half at most.

And she'll come in pooped. She'll probably fall asleep by ten o'clock after she does the dishes, sews on the curtains, and puts the kids to bed. And there I'll be, raring to go.

"Why are you tired all the time?" I asked her last night. She couldn't hear me, not until she switched off the vacuum.

"What did you say?" she answered.

"I said, why are you always tired?"

"I don't know," she admitted.

"You wouldn't be if you went to fitness classes," I said, turning back to my paper.

Quotes my wife can't resist

Of course there are many things about me my wife finds irresistible – my gracefully rounded shoulders, my high (sensitive) forehead, my double-jointed thumb that provides no end of merriment on bleak November nights, my left knee that I can click if the party is getting dull.

However, it's more than a physical attraction.

Jackie also likes the considerate way I hold open doors for her when she's moving heavy furniture; the way I steady her ladder when she's hanging pictures; the way I stack mail on the dining room table on top of my hat, gloves, and coat so as not to take up valuable space in kitchen drawers; the way I never let the children kiss the dog on the mouth until they've washed their faces first; the way . . .

Well, let me just say Jackie is so gosh darn happy that she often expresses her intention never to get married again if anything happens to me.

And I can tell by the way her lip quivers when she says it she isn't kidding.

Having pointed out my good points, I think it only fair to add, however, that there is one thing about me that Mrs. Lautens doesn't like.

It's the way I read to her.

Lately, for example, I've been reading the paperback edition of Lester Pearson's memoirs and every time I come to a part that I really like (which is pretty often) I read it aloud to Jackie.

Last evening, for example, we were in the front room, Jackie going through her favourite daily, yours truly engrossed in Mike Pearson's account of his early days at college, in World War I, and then as a lecturer at University of Toronto.

"Listen to this," I'd say to Jackie, and then launch into a sentence, perhaps a paragraph, but always less than a full page, of the late prime minister's autobiography.

Jackie would look up from what she was reading herself and politely listen. Once or twice she told me not to laugh so much as I read the excerpt, and on one occasion she hinted she'd like me to wait until she finished the particular article she was on.

However, when I interrupted for what I swear was no more than the thirty-seventh time, thirty-eighth if you count the amusing anecdote I related about the time I had lunch with Mr. Pearson, a story my wife hasn't heard for perhaps weeks, well, Mrs. Lautens got pretty huffy.

"Let me finish the paper," she ordered, "or do you want me to start reading interesting things to you out loud, too?"

Of course I was shocked.

To show my disappointment at her attitude, I immediately took my feet out from behind her back where they were getting warm and sat straight up on the chesterfield. I know it was pretty cruel, but a man doesn't like to be stopped when he's in the middle of reciting a really topnotch chapter of a book.

Fortunately, I'm not one to carry a grudge.

Undoubtedly tonight, when I'm back reading the book, I'll give Jackie a second chance to hear me quote particularly clever phrases and guffaw over Lester Pearson's days in Hamilton, or some such. That's the kind of forgiving guy I am.

Maybe I should twist my nose first and make the cartilage pop. That always puts Jackie in a good mood.

Locker room Valentine

Every Valentine's Day my wife surprises me. She surprises me with paper hearts. Paper hearts, you may point out, are not especially surprising. And I agree. But it's where my wife pastes the hearts that catches me by surprise.

Last Valentine's Day, for example, I picked up my electric razor and discovered it swarming with tiny red hearts. The February 14 before that, my typewriter got the heart treatment. Over the years, I've had paper hearts stuck to lunch bags, place mats at the table, my morning newspaper, and even my forehead.

So you can imagine how I felt when Valentine's Day rolled

around this year. I awoke with only one thought: where would Jackie strike this time? I shaved as usual. No hearts on my razor, the bathroom mirror, or my face. At breakfast, the grapefruit checked out and the scrambled eggs were unmarked. The kids were okay. (Yes, she's decorated them, too.) Ditto the dog, the toast, our front door, the tube of toothpaste, my copy paper.

By noon, my nerves were beginning to crack. I knew Jackie had a heart somewhere up her sleeve – but where? Finally I came right out and asked: "Okay, where have you hidden the hearts this year?"

Jackie looked hurt. "That's what's wrong with you," she said, "you're too suspicious."

By the time I left for the Y and my usual little workout, I was ready to agree. Valentine's Day was fast fading – and still no hearts. However, I was half into my gym clothes when the guys in the locker room began to snicker. Then guffaw. I looked down to see the source of their merriment. Yes – Jackie's paper hearts. They were all over my athletic supporter.

If Jackie had to boobytrap my gym equipment, why couldn't she at least have picked on my socks?

Love match I can do without

Mrs. Lautens has signed me up again for tennis lessons, a decision which shows how much faith she has our marriage will last. On my list of favourite things to do, I'd rank tennis about 198th, just behind parachute-jumping, taking a correspondence course in root canal work for fun and profit, and letting a killer shark snatch sardines from between my lips at some marineland extravaganza. Tennis is just not my game.

But Jackie refuses to take my word, claiming deep down I love it. Why is it wives insist they know more about their husband's views on vital topics like tennis, square-dancing, broccoli, and what tie goes best with the brown suit than we do? It's amazing how many times I come to a decision about something only to be corrected by the missus, who tells me that's not how I feel at all.

Anyway, back to tennis. Mrs. Lautens is certain once I learn to hit the ball and serve with a style that doesn't bring Karen Kain in Swan Lake instantly to mind, I'll thank her for signing me up. Of course, she said this the other times she filled out the coupon and sent in the cheque, too, and so far the seething romance (the one I'm supposed to have with tennis) hasn't surfaced.

One thing I have against the game, I think, is the fact tennis players are so picky. Unless you can get the ball back over the net, they don't want to play with you. One or two complete misses and they remember a previous engagement or claim it's time to take an insulin shot or something equally fake.

I wouldn't hazard a guess how many tennis players I've met on the court – once. Let them master the mysteries of the forehand or the complicated business of keeping the ball inside the white lines and they only want to play somebody named Pancho who struts around with four racquets under his arm and a headband above his ears. Snobs.

Tennis gets no marks from me either for being a sport populated with people who look about seventeen years of age and have figures that suggest they wouldn't know a banana cream pie if they swatted it. Who needs the competition? What I'm looking for is a game where a mature man with thin hair, white legs, no reflexes to speak of, and a waist that knows its way to Frank Vetere's pizzeria can look good.

Okay, end of complaining.

This year we're taking lessons for a second time (although he will deny it to anyone who has seen my backhand, a swish followed by a loud, "I'm sorry!") from Peter Dimmer. We didn't even have to use false names to enroll, which indicates he is even-tempered or loves a challenge.

To make sure I didn't run off to Brandon to cover a sewage convention or stop breathing in a clever attempt to convey a saving impression of death, Jackie didn't tell me about our first tennis lesson (last night) until the last possible moment. When I got home, my tennis stuff was laid out and Mrs. Lautens informed we could only have a bowl of chicken soup for dinner because we were due on the court in one hour.

"The last time we had a lesson you had chili for dinner (how can wives remember details like that?) and it upset your stomach," she said. "We'll go light at dinner for the next two weeks while we take our tennis lessons."

Sixty minutes later, I was swinging vainly at a tennis ball and having, what my wife assures me, was the time of my life. Apparently nothing makes me happier than a sore shoulder and gulping for breath.

But to end on a happy note I should point out one thing: the tennis class is split in four groups – the Wimbledons at the top, the Queens at the bottom. Purely out of seniority, the instructor has allowed me to move up to the second-from-bottom group, the Forest Hills. At least when he asks the Queens to stand up this year, I don't have to respond. I'm not insensitive, you know.

It Happens to Everyone

My no-iron wife

My wife hates ironing. Jackie will cook, clean, hang wall-paper, fix plumbing, perform minor surgery, and, in a pinch, wax floors. But the only thing she wants to press around the house is her luck. We have the only steam iron made in 1957 with the original water still inside.

To put it kindly, Jackie has a psychological fear of getting ahead in her ironing. For example, if I drop dead tomorrow, she'll have to rush downstairs and iron a shirt for me for the funeral – only the front, of course.

The last thing Jackie wants to be caught with is an ironed shirt over. Apparently it's a theory. Like Dorian Gray, Jackie believes if my shirts get wrinkled, she won't. So my wife still looks eighteen but somewhere in the basement there's a pair of French cuffs that could pass for 126.

As a result of my wife's anti-ironing philosophy, there's a rumour going round our street that I'm a nudist. That's because whenever the neighbours see me through the windows, I'm naked to the waist. They assume I'm waiting for the sun to come out and the volleyball game to start. However, what I'm really waiting for is a shirt.

Shirts make my wife mad enough to spit, but not on an iron. As you can imagine, Jackie was one of the most enthusiastic supporters of wash-and-wear shirts when they were introduced. She claimed she didn't mind playing beau and Arrows, provided the Arrows were perma-press. So out went the old shirts and in came the new jobs.

However, the miracle fibres aren't all they're cracked up to be either – or so Jackie claims. It's true they don't need iron-ing. Just a touch here and there. But they do break out in fuzz balls, or "pills," which give the shirts a shaggy look. Jackie says the best way to get rid of them is with a razor.

So my closet is still empty. My wife is caught up on her ironing, thanks to the new fabrics. But she's three weeks behind in her shaving.

The world's foremost "A" expert

If I ever get on one of those quiz shows with the fabulous prizes, I don't care what they ask – provided it begins with "A." That's my specialty. In fact, I may be the world's foremost "A" expert.

Abscesses, absinth, accordions, acetylene, and Achilles tendons are no mystery to me. And what I could tell you about adenoids should be worth a trip (for two) to Hawaii or an automobile on any TV game show.

The secret of my expertise when it comes to "A" (A, first letter and first vowel in the English alphabet . . . derived from ancient Semitic script . . .) is simple: my wife can't refuse those encyclopedia "bargains" at the supermarket – the ones that start you off with Volume One (A-Amer) for fifty-nine cents.

Unfortunately, subsequent volumes soar in price, sometimes as high as $2.49 each. Or they appear on store shelves the very week that meat is up, or sugar doubles. In any case, we never get as far as Volume Two; our book case is filled with twenty or thirty encyclopedias – but all Volume One.

Naturally, it's rather limiting. I can locate Aberdare, Aberdeen, Abilene, and Adapazari on any decent map. Not even Lake Agassiz is beyond my grasp, But I haven't a clue where to find Boston, Chile, Davos, or Ecuador, let alone something as remote in the alphabet as Zambia.

Perhaps it's only my imagination, but I also suspect the people who write encyclopedias don't put their best bits in Volume One. They seem to save all the interesting people for the $2.49 volumes. For example, the fifty-nine-cent introductory job never has anything about Shakespeare or Hitler or Rasputin. Instead we get essays on Abd-al-Aziz, sultan of Morocco from 1894-1908; on Niels Abel, 1802-1829, Norwegian mathematician; and on Lascelles Abercrombie, 1881-1938, British poet.

No offence, but those are hardly superstars; their names seldom pop up at cocktail parties where you're trying to make an impression.

But, alas, it's my fate to be forever stuck at the front of the book. Just this past weekend my wife was shopping and picked up (for fifty-nine cents) the first volume in an encyclopedia of wildlife. Of course we will never get to Volume Two, let alone Volume Twenty-Two.

But if anyone wants to know about aardvarks, aardwolfs, abalone, accentor, or addax, I'm your man.

The unkindest cut

The universe may be unfolding as it should but in this fast-changing world there's one thing every man wants to remain the same – his wife's hairstyle.

We can face a new ice age, adapt to population explosions,

even find our way around downtown Toronto when they build a new one every weekend, but God help Mr. Armand when he starts fooling with the missus' bangs. Hubby wants every hair to be in its proper, and usual, place, and that goes for the part, too. For heaven's sake, we all need something to cling to, even if it's just a familiar cowlick or a shade of Miss Clairol we've learned to love over the years.

You can imagine my chagrin, then, when my wife came home the other day with her hair cut short enough to qualify for a YMCA membership. She didn't have enough hair left for a gnat to run barefoot through, let alone a forty-seven-year-old man with size eleven shoes.

"What happened?" I asked, expecting to hear that my wife's head had been caught in the coffee grinder at the supermarket, and that a large settlement was on its way.

Unfortunately, the news wasn't that good.

"I was sitting at the hairdresser's and I decided to change my hair," she said simply.

"After only nineteen years of wearing your hair the same way you decided to change it?" I gasped, unable to believe my ears. "But I liked it the old way."

"This will take less work," was her casual reply.

I was so furious I could have sucked my arm and bruised myself. What a frivolous, selfish, rotten thing to do to me! Jackie's hair was the one constant in my life, and now it's gone!

Worse still, everyone who sees her new hairstyle tells her – now get this – they like it. Even husbands who would put their fingers in an electric outlet and stand in a bucket of water if their wives came home with the same thing.

So far Jackie has been informed the new hair cut makes her look (1) younger, (2) much younger, and (3) young enough to pass for my daughter. I'd be worried about the flattery turning her head if I weren't more concerned about what's outside.

What's next? Wigs, colour rinses, expensive falls, frosted

tips, for God's sake? Where will it end?

I'm not one of those men who wants to nail his wife's foot to the kitchen floor and Crazy Glue a frypan or broom in the palm of her hand. Certainly not. I want my wife's soul to fulfil itself, her spirit to soar free, her mind to challenge the great unsolved problems of mankind. But I wish she'd leave her hair alone.

With my luck, I'll just be getting used to this new hairstyle around 1995, and she'll change it again.

Darling, don't take my side

If my face looks cranky today and the smile definitely forced, it's because of a rather nasty experience I had in bed last night. After twenty years of marriage, the missus came up with the most outlandish suggestion in all our 7,300-plus nights of sleeping together. She wanted to change sides.

Yes, just like that, with no warning, without so much as a "now-don't-get-mad-but," Jackie wanted to change

Of course I was thunderstruck. Since 1957, and room 5 at the Golden Gate Motel near London (Ont.), the left side of the bed has always been mine. There was never any question of that. Whether in Leningrad, Paris, Rome, London, Vienna, or something really exotic like a Day's Inn on the way to Myrtle Beach, that has always been the sleeping arrangement. Me left, Jackie right.

Why this bizarre suggestion to change sides? Because (Jackie claimed) she could feel a draft coming from the register on her

side of the bed. On grounds as flimsy as those, she wanted to tamper with tradition, upset the normal way of doing things, and take my (left) side of the bed. Oh, what fickle creatures women are, changing their minds after a measly decade or two of successful sleeping habits.

Being a gentleman, I agreed to the switch, but I knew the arrangement would never work. A confirmed left-side-of-the-bed sleeper cannot be bounced around and still zonk out before he gets to the third sheep.

Of course I was right. First off, I stretched out my left foot, expecting as usual to find nothing but a lot of empty space. Instead, it collided with another foot – my wife's – which normally wouldn't be there. What a start that gives you, especially when it's dark and your left foot has enjoyed over twenty years of comparative freedom and an occasional dangle over the side of the bed.

It's also jarring for a left-side-of-the-bed sleeper to turn on his left shoulder and suddenly come face to face with another face, a face your subconscious tells you should be on the other side.

Changing bed sides in mid-marriage is just asking for trouble, if you ask me. How can you possibly get the necessary eight hours when the clock-radio appears to have drifted to the other side of the room and what you push down in your stupor to see the time is your wife's nose? How can you keep your good temper and drift off for a snore when you reach over for the customary goodnight kiss and fall out on the floor instead? For heaven's sake, how can anyone climb into the arms of Morpheus when he knows, if he has to go to the bathroom in the middle of the night, he may make his usual turn and wind up in a closet by mistake, with unfortunate results?

No, it's wrong and, after almost two hours of tossing and turning on the wrong (right) side of the bed, I had to shake my wife and tell her to give back my proper side. She'd have to put up with the draft. Which she did with some fuss, I might add, and an elbow I don't altogether consider an accident.

So I am two hours' short in my sleep today, and grumpy.

Instead of all that business of "love, honour, and cherish" in the marriage ceremony, I knew I should have got Jackie to promise me the left side of the bed, 'til etc., etc.

She may forget a name but . . .

Jackie has a real knack for forgetting names. Whenever she meets someone, old friend or new, the thing she usually finds on the tip of her tongue is her foot. Names just elude her. First names, family names, nicknames – names.

To my wife, every one has the same name – "there" as in, "Hi, there!" Mind you, she also forgets telephone numbers, how to get to places she's been, what time the kids said they'd be home for supper, and if she turned the stove off.

But Jackie does have a good memory when it comes to dresses. In fact, I'd say she has total dress recall. Mention any wine and cheese reception, Sunday brunch, office party, sit-down dinner, or birthday bash in the past two decades, and Jackie can tell you what dress she wore. More impressive, she can tell you what the other women there wore, too.

How can it be? Here's a person who can't remember she put buns in the oven to heat up an hour and a half ago, but she knows instantly she was wearing her mauve dress (the one with the mandarin collar) the last time we had dinner with Isobel and George in 1974. Oh, yes, and that Isobel had on her blue Ports suit, a white blouse, and a bracelet with twenty-three charms.

Jackie may boob on a brooch or miss an accessory like a belt, but when it comes to the big stuff – cocktail dresses, pantsuits, evening gowns, wedding rings – she has total recall.

Before we go out for the evening, my wife likes to know who may be there so she can pick her wardrobe accordingly. Heaven knows she's no clothes horse. Some of Jackie's things date back to high school days. But she lives in dread that one of the dinner guests may go home saying, "Jackie Lautens wore that same outfit the last time we saw her, too." That, apparently, is my wife's concept of Hell. So she has developed this fantastic ability to remember exactly what she was wearing the last time she met "what's-his-name" or even "what's-his-name's wife."

Is it a trick memory? I pride myself on having some sort of talent for recollecting the past, but I couldn't for the life of me tell you what I was wearing the last time we were at a party together. It was either my blue suit, or my brown one, but I couldn't tell you which.

Even more amazing than Jackie's phenomenal memory is the reaction I get when I tell people about it. The other day I mentioned to a woman at the office how Jackie can recall perfectly what she had on at every social gathering we've ever attended.

"Can you imagine anyone knowing what she wore to all those parties, and what the other women were wearing, too?" I asked.

"Certainly," the woman replied. "Doesn't everyone?"

Well, the men I talked to were astonished.

The washer socks it to me

My cousin Diana has some pretty strong views about socks. Men's socks. According to Diana, no matter how many socks you put in a washer, you always get one less out. Diana has put socks in washers in Winnipeg, Toronto, New York and in Chicago where she and her husband Morley (and two children) now live and it never fails. Dump in twelve socks and eleven come out; sixteen become fifteen; eight become seven; well, the number doesn't matter.

What is happening across the world is that the supply of men's socks is reduced by one sock every time somebody does a load of wash.

Diana has no theory about what happens to the sock in question but she knows it isn't a matter of which detergent you use. She's tried them all and the effect is invariably the same. The obvious conclusion is that washers are designed to consume one sock every time they're turned on, but Diana is willing to leave explanations to science.

Her chief concern can be summed up in a few words: what are you supposed to do with the surviving sock of a pair? Her off-the-top answer is a sock exchange. Diana figures the newspaper should have a page put aside for readers interested in matching up all the single socks they've got at the bottom of their laundry baskets.

As she sees it, a person could list surviving hosiery in a notice like this: "Available for immediate occupancy, one black cushion-sole sock (ankle-length), one executive gray polyester-and-cotton sock (calf length), one Argyle sock in showroom condition, one sports sock with fewer than twenty miles on it, one subdued patterned sock used only to walk to church Sunday. Can you match or deal? Reply Box 999."

Diana feels such a sock exchange would serve a real need in

the community and get the solitary footwear of the country moving again. People are so desperate to find a solution to the problem, Diana feels, they wouldn't object to wearing somebody else's sock if the thirty or forty unmatched socks in the typical closet can be transformed into fifteen or twenty usable pairs.

Until the sock exchange becomes a reality, Diana is trying an experiment. She has started buying her husband socks with little dome fasteners near the cuff. Before dunking them in hot suds, Diana simply snaps them together and, while she still loses one regular sock per wash, so far none of the snapped-together pairs has gone missing.

My own wife attacks the problem more directly. Jackie restricts me to identical black, elastic-top socks so that I've always got a matching pair, at least until I'm down to one sock. And she stitches a thread of blue wool in the cuff so she can separate mine from our sons'.

There are no flies on girls from Hamilton Beach.

Sit-ups in bed, Honey?

The big problem with having had only one wife is not having anyone to compare her with. For example, is it normal for a woman to do exercises every morning in bed? Under the covers? Usually while her husband is still trying to catch that last valuable wink of sleep? That is how it is at our house.

Moments after the alarm has gone off, there is a great writhing and thumping, bouncing and kerplunking on our

Beautyrest. Jackie is doing her daily dozens again. She does sit-ups, knee twists, leg raises; she touches elbow to knee; she crosses her hands back and forth like a semaphore signaller on a sinking ship; she rotates her head. In short, Mrs. Lautens leaves no sternum untouched.

And, as I mentioned earlier, she goes through all this while still under our duvet. That's because, as she explains, it's too cold to do exercises in the bedroom itself, especially on the floor. Hence her choice of gym.

Anyone dropping into the little scene from another planet would naturally assume what was going on under the blankets was an athletic event, or worse. But it's only Jackie.

Frankly, if I get caught in bed during one of her exercise sessions, I can develop motion sickness very quickly. It's like having a team of Swedish trampoline artists for a bedmate.

But Jackie insists what she is doing is perfectly natural and not unusual at all. How can I argue? It's like when she tells me ironing is only a rumour started by busybody women who like to make trouble. Or that a thick layer of dust on the furniture preserves the wood and makes end tables last a lot longer. Or that taking off your shoes when you come into the house is proper behaviour, even if you do slide in your socks and fall down the stairs a lot. Or that kissing and fooling around when the kids are out causes warts. Or that men who can get an extra day out of a shirt go to heaven faster than men who don't. Or . . .

Well, there's quite a long list of things Jackie has told me in the twenty-three years of our married life, including the one that if a wife doesn't get to Myrtle Beach for a holiday at least once every other year, the husband goes impotent.

Anyway, with only one wife to my name, how can I tell if Mrs. Lautens is acting like a perfectly normal member of that honourable profession? Do all married women tap dance in the kitchen during breakfast and sing, over and over, the first three words only of every song lyric ever written? Do they all have freezer compartments in their refrigerators with items that may have been there dead a decade, or longer? Do they all consider having their back scratched part of a husband's regular chores and give you a dirty look if you stray even the slightest off course? Do they all want to hammer 13,000 holes in the walls to hang up pictures? Do they all whip up the thermostat when nobody's looking?

Do they, to conclude on the same inquiring note we started, do they all do exercises at 7 a.m., under the covers, in cosy bed?

Those people who have been to the altar, or other, several times may have a quick answer, but when your experience is limited to one (1), the best you can manage is a profound shrug.

The great crockery caper

Life can surely hold no more thrills for Mrs. Lautens. The Resident Love Goddess has reached a personal Everest that makes all else pale in comparison.

Let me put it this way. Jackie wouldn't trade what happened this past week for a date with Robert Redford, a guarantee from Bjorn Bjorg to help with her backhand, drinkie-poos with Ken Thomson and a tour of his wallet, or the name of a hairdresser who doesn't lean. What took place in the past seven days is even better (in her estimation) than having a burglar break into the house and steal her iron.

Okay, no more suspense. This past week my wife went out and bought a new set of kitchen dishes. For the first time in twenty-three years of marriage, we now have dinnerware that actually matches! The dinner plates are all the same, likewise the bread-and-butters, the tea plates, salad bowls, cups and saucers. Even more breathtaking, there aren't any chips out of the crockery. This is brand new, grade A stuff.

Practically since day one of our life together, Jackie has had a dream, a dream that we would one day have kitchen dishes that didn't look like leftovers from an Animal House movie.

I said she might just as well dream of winning Loto Canada or even coming home just once after the kids have made their own supper and finding the kitchen clean. Nobody, I pointed out, ever has fewer than the remnants of four patterns of kitchen dishes on the go, and to have three dinner plates and two nappes that match at the same time (our best previous record set in 1974) is about as much as any couple with a family can hope for.

The words didn't deter Jackie. We kept eating from surviving dishes of a wedding set given us by cousin June, on dinnerware retired from active service by relatives and no longer wanted, from plates that came with detergent ("Bonus Inside!"), from cereal bowls the gift of grateful service stations after a spring special, oil change and lube job. And there were other saucers and the like whose history had been long lost in the mists of time.

But amid the cream plates with maroon flowers, the blue ones with stylized chickens, the bowls with the bear cubs on the bottom, etc., my wife kept the faith.

About a week ago, a department store had a special on kitchen dishes and, without telling any one, Jackie ordered a full six-place setting. She felt we were at last mature enough to handle matching dinnerware with smooth edges.

When we sat at the kitchen table that evening, the new stuff was laid out in snowy splendour. There wasn't a crack in sight. Believe me, it was an emotional moment. Jackie was so choked up she barely could say, "Anyone break one of these new dishes and I'll kill them."

Where the old stuff has gone I don't know, probably into

the basement where it will stay until one of our kids goes off on his own and needs a starter set(s).

In the meantime, it's pretty elegant dining off kitchen dishes that are the same colour, shape, and design. Of course, our kitchen glasses still don't match. However, I don't think even Jackie dreams that big.

Cave space rearranged

I don't know of any words that strike more terror in a grown man's heart than the ones Mrs. Lautens whispered over the telephone the other day. There I was at the office, minding somebody else's business, which is a journalist's regular line of work, when the main woman in my life called and said: "I've rearranged the furniture in the front room."

It was devastating. If she had informed me our daughter had run off with a tag team of touring midget wrestlers, I would have felt awful. If she had stated our son was toying with the idea of buying a suitcase-size radio and walking down the street with it turned full blast to CHUM, I would have been terribly depressed. But rearranging the furniture in the front room? That is definitely going too far.

A man likes his front room to stay the way it is. He wants to come home after a hard day in the trenches, throw himself down, and be reasonably certain of landing on a chesterfield. He does not want to find himself sitting on a magazine rack with the TV guide poking up his never-you-mind.

Is that too much to ask of life?

Apparently.

Jackie adores switching furniture, even though our front room is only nine feet wide, twelve if you count the hallway, which really is cheating.

What caused this latest rearrangement of the life goods is a pew purchased (for $40) from our church, which is in the process of being torn down, sob. Mrs. Lautens wanted a souvenir of St. Andrew's, the one on Bloor St. near Church, where our children have spent many an hour pretending to sing hymns, especially Richard.

So off we had trotted, Père Lautens and the two male offspring, to unbolt the pew and bring it home under the watchful supervision of Foreperson Jackie.

(Where, I ask, are the libbers when it comes time to get on a dusty floor and reach behind a radiator to wrestle with a screw covered with 78 layers of shellac and driven in crooked by the world's strongest human being?)

Of course, I thought that would be the end of the suffering part, but when Mrs. Lautens got the pew into its planned spot (our hallway), she decided next day only a complete reshuffle of our belongings would do.

I whimpered and whined when I got the news over the telephone, pleading with the missus not to give me another of her patented surprises, the kind that cause the few hairs left on my head to sit down and write suicide notes.

It was to no avail, however. Everything, as threatened, was changed around. The sectional chesterfield has been broken up, the bamboo bench and matching chair are in the kitchen with a plant (they have become part of the resident decorator's "tropicana" motif), and whenever I get up from the purple chair I bump my head on a lamp that wasn't there before.

The personal cave sure isn't what it used to be in the good old days, about a week ago.

I'm afraid the old church pew is hearing language it never

heard before, but how would you like to automatically put down a cup and find you've missed the coffee table by four feet?

Spaghetti tradition cut short

All of us in the Lautens household are facing the cruel fact that one of our great family traditions has been laid to rest forever. Never again, it seems, will Jackie cook too much spaghetti for dinner.

For nearly twenty-five years Mrs. Lautens has prepared too much spaghetti for the eager faces around our dinner table. It's something we could count on.

Jackie can size up any crowd in rice pudding, gauge a platoon if necessary in hamburg patties, make the french fries work out to the final fry. But spaghetti has been her downfall since she first learned the mysteries of that delicious food from Danny Pugliese's mother in Welland.

For some reason, when my wife looks at spaghetti before dumping same in boiling water, she invariably comes to the same conclusion: there isn't enough. So she plops in more. As a result, we've always wound up with enough leftover spaghetti to feed the entire cast of a Puccini opera, plus every citizen of the city of Naples whose family name ends in "i."

At a guess, I'd say we have spaghetti once a week, or fifty-two times a year. Even calculated at twenty years, that works out to 1,040 spaghetti dinners that Mrs. Lautens has over-estimated. And not once has the Sun of my Life come even close to getting the amount right. (When you're exposing a woman's spaghetti faults, a little flattery never hurts.) In short, her record is 0-1,040, with not even a tie.

Invariably, after every spaghetti dinner, Mrs. Lautens looks at the bowl in the middle of the table, still heaped high enough to challenge Steve Podborski in a cup downhill, and begs: "Can't anyone help out?" To eat even another mouthful at that point would be dangerous to everyone's health, not to mention the brickwork, so we always decline, leaving Mrs. Lautens to vow that next time will be different. But it isn't.

As I say, this has been going on throughout our married life, but at Christmas our Richard gave his mother a special present – a spaghetti measurer.

The little plastic gadget cost less than $3 and Jackie used it for the first time last evening. She put in what the measurer claimed was the right amount of spaghetti for five people and, what do you know, it came out dead on. Stephen, Jane, Richard, Jackie, and I each had just the right amount of spaghetti – and there wasn't a single strand left in the bowl!

Mrs. Lautens was really pleased with herself as we cleared the table, commenting that not having spaghetti left over was a new and wonderful experience. For the first time she wouldn't have to put spaghetti in the refrigerator for two or three days, and then throw it out. (Throwing it out immediately offends her sense of thrift.)

Naturally, we're happy about Jackie's triumph, too, although it's always sad to see any family tradition bite the dust. I wonder how long it will be before Richard asks for seconds, just to see the panic on his mother's face when she looks at an empty spaghetti bowl.

In Sickness and in Health

First "ah," then "ugh!"

It's been my philosophy not to tamper with something that's running properly, more or less, so I have never had a medical.

I realize it's naughty of me. As they say in the brochures, you should have a doctor tap on your knees once a year, shine a bright light in your eye, and assure you as he flops you over on one side, "Relax. This will only take a minute."

But I am basically a shy lad who surrenders his knickers only with a fight. I just cannot pull off the scene where the nurse tells you to be a brave boy and sticks the needle in your finger, nor am I cool at that moment of crisis when you stand there, silly grin from ear to ear, with a specimen bottle in your hand.

Of course I realize it's all in the interest of science, but it's just not for me. If God had meant us to go around starkers, I believe, he wouldn't have given us Eaton's. That, as I say, has been my sunny approach to life for forty-nine (can you believe it?) years.

However, the missus decided recently it would be a good idea to see how many miles were left on the old liver, and if it was time to rotate my kidneys. When you don't have a good black dress to your name, you take these precautions. So she made an appointment with the family doctor (whom I had never met) to examine me from stem to gudgeon even though, I assure you, I have never had any problem with either, especially my gudgeon.

The appointment was for Tuesday afternoon and I took special care to arrive in mint condition – fresh socks, just laundered undershorts, wax-free ears, underarms with twenty-four-hour protection. I did not want to make a bad first impression.

The doctor was the soul of courtesy and said right off the

top that he had a lot of husbands come in for medicals ordered by their wives. Apparently many women can't determine whether their husbands are alive or not, especially on weekends, and would like a second opinion, preferably one from a person who is a college graduate.

In the next hour I breathed, coughed, touched my toes, and did all the other things expected of me while the good doctor examined my moving parts, and poked the non-moving with a stick. At the end of the session he pronounced me fit except for a mild case of sloped shoulders, a physical problem caused by hunching over a typewriter these many years while putting the world right on Important Issues.

Yes, healthy, he said, with innards (and outards) good for another fifty or sixty years of normal wear and tear.

While walking home I had to admit to myself that the missus was right again. It was a good idea to have the various bits and pieces put under the probing eye of the medical profession, and certified. What a feeling of confidence it gives! What a sense of vim and vitality! What inner strength!

At precisely 11:30 that evening I was draped over the plumbing in the bathroom, sick as the legendary dog.

Flu.

Well, for almost six hours I was perfect.

Faith in my thermometer

When I get sick, I make a beeline for the medicine chest – and our friendly family thermometer. I like to take my temperature. I take it at the drop of a symptom; I take it if my tongue looks pale; I take it when there's a bad weather report in the newspaper. But I take it. That's because I have great faith in my temperature.

Don't misunderstand. I'm no hypochondriac. I never watch Trapper John, M.D., on TV. I prefer steak to vitamin E. And I wouldn't let even Hawkeye Pierce take out my gall bladder without a second opinion. But I do like to operate at a steady 98.6 degrees. Who cares what the Mayo boys say? Just where is the mercury in that little tube of glass? That's my guide.

Having explained that, you can understand how concerned I was a few days ago when I got home from work and announced I was dying.

"Where's the thermometer?" I asked. "I've got a headache, my throat's sore, and I don't think I'll last out the day."

"The kids broke it," my wife replied.

"Broke it!" I exploded. "I'm at death's door and you tell me we don't have a thermometer! This is terrible."

"Relax – and get into bed," my wife advised. "I'll bring in the TV, get you a drink . . ."

"There may not be time," I whispered. "Look, I want my cuff links to go to Stephen; Richard gets my watch; and Jane can have . . ."

"Don't be so dramatic," I was informed. "All you've got probably is a touch of the flu."

"How do you know?" I challenged. "It could be something awful. And we'll never know unless we take my temperature."

My wife finally got me settled in and for three days I didn't stir. At last my nerves crumbled.

"I can't stand not knowing how close to the end I am," I shouted. "I've got to get to a thermometer." With that I began rummaging through every drawer in the house.

Ten minutes later I was triumphant. "I found a thermometer in the bathroom cupboard," I said.

"But . . ." my wife began.

I popped the thermometer in my mouth.

"Oh, never mind," she sighed.

After a suitable interval, I pulled the thermometer from under my tongue. "See – 99.2," I said. "By the way, what were you saying a minute ago?"

"I was just going to say that's the thermometer I use for the dog," my wife said.

Funny, there were no teeth marks on it.

The flu almost killed me

Flu is always a rotten business, but there's a strain making the rounds this winter that, if you're not careful, can lead to a rather nasty case of death. I know because I've just had it.

Yes, the Grim Reaper has been pulling on the drawstring of my jammies, and my end has been in sight, several times. However, here I am, almost alive, and practically well.

But make no mistake. Just two hours ago I was on the verge, ready to order the solid imitation mahogany slumber box with brass simulated plastic handles, sateen lining, and wax lily spray.

Yes, I thought I was a goner.

What was so frightening was the suddenness with which the crisis came. There I was, lying in bed, as I have a dozen times with the flu, watching daytime TV, reading magazines, sucking candies, and looking at the dreadful weather outside. I remember shouting downstairs to my wife, "Has the mail come yet?" And she responded, "You just asked twelve seconds ago and the answer is still no."

At that moment I felt a little headachey, perhaps stuffed up, but there was certainly no hint that I should gather the children 'round me and start handing out cufflinks or dividing up my silver dollar collection.

Next I shouted, "What are you doing?"

"The dishes," Jackie answered. "This is the fifteenth time you've asked this morning what I'm doing."

"I just like to know," I hollered down the stairs. "Do you know where the TV guide is? I think there's an old movie on I'd like to see."

A minute later Jackie came up the stairs with the guide and threw it on the bed. "Is that what you want?" she asked.

"I wish you'd tell me when you're coming upstairs," I chided. "I'd have asked you to bring me something to drink."

"Have you finished the lemonade I brought you three minutes ago?"

"Yes."

"I'll make some iced tea and bring that the next time I'm coming up," she promised.

"Who was that on the phone just now?" was my next question.

"Andrea. She wants me to come over for lunch, but I told her you were in bed with the flu and we'd have to put it off a day or so."

"Would you take my temperature?" I suggested.

"I took it a couple of hours ago."

"How about a back rub?"

Jackie agreed and went to the bathroom to get the rubbing alcohol. "I know you have to blow your nose," she said when she got back to the bedroom, "but can't you put the old Kleenex in the wastebasket after you've finished?"

"I was playing basketball and I missed," I said.

After the back rub, Jackie said, "Can I get back to my work now?"

"Sure, but can you adjust the TV better before you go, and

straighten the bed? It's kind of lumpy, and the crumbs from the sandwich bother me."

Jackie did exactly that, plumped up my pillow, put the wastebasket next to the bed, took away the empty glasses, and went downstairs.

"Was that the mailman?" I yelled what must have been at least four or five minutes later.

"No," Jackie said, shrilly.

"What are you doing now?"

"Talking to you, but I want to go down to the basement to do some ironing."

"Don't forget my drink," I bellowed, "and maybe a cold cloth for my . . ."

That's when the crisis in my illness struck, when I went right to the brink, when the River Styx practically lapped at my tootsies.

"If you don't go back to work soon, I'll kill you," the missus vowed from the foot of the stairs.

Whether this is a common side-effect of the flu, I don't know, but I consider myself lucky to be here (at the office), and in one piece. I wonder if *Reader's Digest* is interested in my dice with Death?

Suffering in silence

The scene is your bed. It's three o'clock in the morning. You've got a cold. Your nose is plugged. Your head hurts. And you can't sleep. In short, you're at death's door, or at least on the sidewalk.

But what really bugs you? What really bugs you, my friend, is your wife. There she is at your side – sleeping like a baby. You could be ready to turn up your toes, for heaven's sake, and she'd never know. The snore in her sinuses would drown out any rattle your throat could muster. It's an awful moment.

Frankly, I can take a little sickness now and then, but I'll be darned if I'll suffer in silence. You are not looking at a man who wants to hide his blight under a bushel. Where does it say I have to be a hero? Look, I want an audience when I've got the heaves. I absolutely refuse to throw up unless somebody's there to lend encouragement, not to mention a cold cloth. It's sympathy I want, not solitude, especially at three o'clock in the morning.

Alas, it's one of fate's cruel tricks that while I have been linked in life with a lovely creature with a sweet disposition, she also happens to sleep like a stone. You'd be astonished at what I have to go through to make sure she realizes I'm not getting a wink of sleep. I fluff up my pillow. I turn a hundred times. I sneeze into her ear. I choke and throw in an assortment of sneezes. Even then, I often have to turn on the bathroom light and let it shine in her face before she snaps out of her slumber.

That's not the end of it. Usually, her first words are, "What's wrong, honey?"

Naturally, I reply, "Nothing."

"Oh," she answers – and then goes back to sleep again.

Can you imagine that? How can she accept the word of a man who obviously is out of his mind with fever? Unless I flush the toilet a few times, trip over the dog, or bump into furniture, she never gets up.

Being sick is certainly tiring work if you're married to a sound sleeper.

Having the sniffles
with Jackie at work

A lot of fun has gone out of being sick around our place since Mrs. Lautens decided to take a part-time job.

In the good old days, when you caught something dreadful, it was wonderful to have someone ask how you were feeling, hold your forehead in a caring hand, say how brave you were to take the medicine, puff up any unpuffed pillows, race up and down the stairs with hot drinks, etc.

But last week your agent got a cold and the only company he had, poor lamb, was Phil Donahue on the bedroom TV. Somehow it wasn't the same. As far as I can recall, this is the first time I've ever been sick on my own and it's an experience I hope I never have to go through again.

Of course, it will bring tears to your eyes but just picture the cruel scene: there I was (practically at death's door, if you ask me) stretched out in bed with no one to gasp at my sneezes, no one to comment on how pale I was, no one to reprimand me when I got up to go to the bathroom without putting on my socks. Believe me, I had to do even the slightest things for myself. It was awful.

The low point came, however, when I had to say, "Toot, toot, here comes the choo-choo!" as I gave myself a spoon of cough syrup. A sick person should not have to say, "Toot, toot!" to himself. Besides, it's hard to talk and swallow at the same time.

Frankly, if you don't have somebody to straighten the sheets, bring up the mail three seconds after you hear it come through the front door, and suggest you take another day off work, what's the point of being sick? How can anyone enjoy bad health if he has to go downstairs to find his own magazines, heat up his own chicken soup, rub his own chest, or find out what's making all the noise on the street?

Of course, when Mrs. Lautens got home, she tried to make it up by listening extra hard whenever I coughed and saying helpful things like, "When you get a cold, you really get a cold, don't you?" However, nobody can crowd in as much sympathy in a few after-dinner hours as she can in a full day of waiting on a sick person, hand and foot. I bet I didn't call Jackie thirty-five times from the moment she got home 'til we went to bed.

And going to bed was another story. Mrs. Lautens toyed with the idea of sleeping in the back bedroom but I said I had been alone all day and that so far my cold had been a complete bust. So Jackie finally agreed to sleep in our bedroom, provided I stayed on my side, and breathed away from her. She was too busy at the office to catch my cold. After tossing and turning just enough to let Mrs. Lautens know how sick I was, I finally fell asleep for no more than eight hours, my cold being that bad.

Anyway, after being sick in an empty house, I decided to get well today and come to work, where I can be ignored by professionals. Unless my wife decides to quit her job, I don't think I'm going to get sick again. It's just a waste of time.

Noses are red, violets are blue, I had a cold, and now so do you

Is there any guilt worse than that of knowing you've passed

on your cold to someone else, especially a loved one? I think not.

The nasty germs that inhabited my vitals last week have moved on and set up residence in the throat, chest, and other organs of the missus. And I am ashamed. I can hardly face myself in the shaving mirror each morning, so consumed with remorse am I.

Hear that coughing coming from the bedroom? Yes, the sound that resembles a '68 Chev pickup truck turning over on a sub-zero morning. Well, I'm responsible.

Only a few short days ago, there was a healthy human being with sinuses clear as sewer pipe and a forehead cool enough to keep the oleo on. And now look. Eyes puffed, nose the colour of a trombone player's cheeks after a Sousa medley, mouth slightly open to provide the lungs with the necessary oxygen. Usually a vision of loveliness with the haunting sort of profile that drives men mad with desire, Mrs. Lautens this week looks like a boiled lobster. Poor devil!

What have I wrought? Was it the kiss on the forehead I insisted on during the height of my fever, the one I demanded "to make the bad germs go away," that did her in? In the midst of a 3 a.m. coughing fit, did I blow clear my nasal passages with a mighty snort and let some villainous virus elude my Kleenex and escape to Jackie's side of the bed? Or did I leave my glass on the kitchen counter instead of in the sink as instructed?

It doesn't matter now. A cherished person has common respiratory infection, and it's entirely my fault. I brought it home.

Twenty-one years ago I promised love and affection and the occasional giggle after the lights were out. At no time did I mention in the marriage contract a runny nose and a throat you could sand end tables on.

My conscience is in absolute tatters.

To see the poor thing hunched over the stove, making dinner, fills me with sadness. It can't be much fun staring into a pot of bubbling chili when your head feels like a nuclear test site and your stomach is a bit off. Watching Jackie vacuum yesterday with bits of paper stuffed up her nose to keep the carpet dry was such a traumatic experience for me, I had to leave the room.

I realize now I should have insisted she move to the chesterfield in the TV room while my own cold raged in all its juicy splendour, but I can't sleep alone. Besides, when I toss and turn, I need some one to ask, "Are you all right?"

Heaven knows I'm paying for my mistake now. Every time my wife sneezes or reaches for the Aspirin, my heart drops a mile. I recognize immediately those cold symptoms are my old ones, and feel just awful.

To spare my wife the hell I'm going through, I've asked her to breathe the other way, save her hugs for later, sterilize her knives and forks after meals, and to keep the coughing down to a minimum while she's waxing floors or moving heavy furniture.

Guilt is a terrible thing and I wouldn't want her to catch that, too.

My thoughtfulness cures her cold

The recuperative powers of the female are truly amazing. Last evening when I got home, the missus was complaining mightily about a cold. Her throat was sore; her head ached; her nasal passages felt like day-old spaghetti. The poor dear had to struggle through dinner and I warned the children not to add to her burden by asking for seconds. I even went so far as to order them out of the kitchen while Jackie cleared up. No one can say I'm an uncaring husband who leaves the children underfoot while the sick loved one loads the dishwasher, wipes the counter, wraps the leftovers in plastic, bundles the garbage, and makes sure everything's turned off.

No, thanks to my insistence, Stephen, Jane, and Richard watched TV upstairs with me, thus leaving my wife a clear path to the chores. I'm certain my efforts don't go unnoticed either. Jackie is very aware of kindness.

Anyway, after tidying up, my wife said she was going to lie down for a little while, and that is precisely what she did. For almost two hours. During the entire time I kept the volume on the TV set as low as possible so as not to disturb Mrs. Lautens. Except for asking if we had any apples, how she was feeling, and if she remembered to pay the Hydro bill, I didn't disturb her once.

She did answer the telephone in the bedroom twice, but those were calls for the children so I don't feel responsible for that.

Later Jackie did get up for an hour or two (she was afraid she wouldn't sleep through the night if she didn't) but I insisted she get back into bed just after 11 o'clock, which is the usual time we turn in. I even turned my face the other way in bed so she wouldn't breathe into it and feel guilty if I happened to catch her virus. What is a marriage if it isn't based on thoughtfulness?

Sad to say, by morning Jackie's cold didn't seem much better. I told her not to do her exercises before making our breakfasts because it was too much for her, and Jackie said I was probably right. I told her she should crawl right back into bed after she made the kids their lunches, fed the dog, and got us all on our way. To heck with crawling out on the third-floor roof (the dormer in Richard's room) and trying to find the leak that gave us so much trouble during the last storm.

That sort of thing can always wait to a day when she's feeling better.

Well, when I left for the office, I just patted Jackie on the shoulder and told her to take it easy because she sure looked awful. Needless to say, I was pretty concerned, so around noon I telephoned to see how my wife was feeling. My son Stephen answered and said that his mother wasn't home.

"There's a sale on over at The Bay," he told me, "and Mom decided to go over and get a few things."

Well, there you have it. One minute Jackie is practically at death's door, and then next she's well enough to go shopping.

It just goes to show how a wife and mother can bounce back if she gets the proper attention.

Feeling sick over being ill

Mrs. Lautens was sick last week. Dizzy, headachey, queasy stomach, enough circles around her eyes to fill a geometry text. Flu, I suppose. Anyway, Jackie wanted me to call the office and tell them she wouldn't be able to make it to work.

Now, while Jackie was definitely not fit to do all the clever things she's paid to do, there was nothing wrong with her mouth. She could have made the call herself. But she wouldn't.

At our house we operate under the philosophy if you are well enough to call in sick, you should be at work.

Of course it's nuts.

You could have a truck run over your foot, be bitten on the bum by a cobra, pick up a bit of sharp glass in your hand, wrench your back in a fall off the veranda, or ever so many things, and still be able to move your lips well enough to say you are under the weather and staying home. We understand that, but we still want another member of the family to make the call to the boss.

I'm exactly the same. If I stay away from work, I feel terribly guilty. Why, there I am, enjoying myself with all kinds of rotten medicine, a temperature of 102, and an ache in my stomach that I'm sure is serious, when I should be at my work station. For shame! I'm sure it's my Methodist background.

Anyway, in all my years as a member of the work force, I've never called in sick for myself. I leave that to the next-of-kin but, in a pinch, I'm sure I'd even stop a passerby and ask him or her to call my office in an emergency, like my being struck by a bolt of lightning.

To get back to Jackie's flu, after I made the call, the Resident Love Goddess wanted to know what they said. "They said for you to take care of yourself and not rush back before you're well," I told her, as I have on similar occasions in the past.

"You didn't sound too happy, did you, or make any wisecracks?"

"I sounded exactly like a husband with a wife sick-enough-to-stay-home-from-the-office should sound," I guaranteed.

Satisfied her employer realized her illness was genuine, Jackie then curled up in the covers and slept for the rest of the day.

On the day she started feeling better, I suggested Jackie should go outside and take a little walk in the fresh air. "It will do you good."

"Are you crazy?" the flu victim said. "What if somebody sees me, somebody from the office, I mean? They'll think I'm faking."

It didn't matter that Mrs. Lautens still looked pale, or that she hadn't missed a day in over a year at that job, or that everyone is entitled to at least go around the block before plunging back into the daily routine. No, Jackie wouldn't leave the house until she was heading to the office.

She went back to work today very concerned she might look too healthy for somebody who has just taken two days off work. I told her she still looked pretty shaky, definitely not 100 per cent.

That pleased her a lot.

No Sex Please . . .
We're Married

Mama Bear's nightie

I'm not one to complain but I did blow my top the other evening when my wife came to bed.

"Where are you going?" I said as she walked into the bedroom.

"To bed," she announced.

"I thought you might be going to the North Pole," I commented.

"What do you mean by a crack like that?" she wanted to know.

"I mean you're dressed as if you're going to the North Pole. You look like Smokey the Bear."

"You never used to talk that way."

"You never used to dress that way," I answered.

For those of you who weren't there to see for yourself, I must describe my Aphrodite as she climbed into bed. She was wearing a pink nightgown (flannelette) which hung down to her toes and was generous enough to make a lovely awning. On her feet she had wool socks and on her head there was a net. Underneath it all, well, your guess is as good as mine.

"Where's your dog team?" I muttered.

"What's that supposed to mean?"

"Nothing. It's just that the last time I saw anybody dressed like that he was behind a dog sled," I said. "Or was he pulling it?"

"Can I help it if I get cold feet?" she stated.

"Up to your ears?"

"Yes, up to my ears, Mr. Wise Guy. Why don't you save your nasty remarks for your reader. Or do you have two of them now?

"You look like a clothing drive," I insisted.

"If you didn't keep this place so darn cold during the night

I wouldn't have to wear all this stuff," my wife countered. "If you weren't so cheap you'd turn up the furnace a little higher."

"It's healthier around 60 degrees," I said.

"Only if you're a sirloin steak," she countered. "Or a rump roast." And here she gave me a withering glance, which I ducked, of course.

"Whatever happened to that nice blue nightie you had?" I asked.

"That was seven years ago," she said. "It's a cleaning rag now. Besides, when I get up in the middle of the night with the kids, I want to be warm."

"But you don't wear that much clothing when you go to church," I protested. "Has the romance gone from our marriage?"

"It has until spring – or you turn up the furnace," she admitted.

So we just sat there, staring at each other, my wife unwilling to admit she was wrong.

"Supposing, just supposing, we turned up the furnace a little higher at night," I finally said when it appeared that bribery, not logic, would carry the day. "Would you get rid of about ten pounds of what you're wearing and come to bed in something more feminine?"

"Try it and see," she whispered, pulling one sock tantalizingly off a toe.

The next night the furnace was set at an expensive 70 degrees when my wife said she was going to get ready for bed. In a few minutes she reappeared wearing a white negligee, all frills and laces and tiny straps.

"Well?" she asked.

"Come closer," I ordered.

She did.

We looked into each other's eyes. She into mine. Mine into hers.

Finally I spoke.

"How much did it cost?" I asked.

I think it was the wrong thing to say. Or maybe she was planning to wear the wool socks to bed with her new negligee anyway.

Never too late to celebrate

Each autumn there is a social event called The University Homecoming. The Old Grad returns to his alma mater to savor the past, to cheer once more for the Football Twelve, to revive spirits jaded by a world of annual reports and graphs and ugly profits, to drink deeply again from the fountain of learning – oh, yes, especially that. Some swallow so eagerly they cannot move by halftime and must be carried home.

It's good to get away from sordid business, to rejoin the academic life where, except for an annual pledge, a donation to the library fund, a gift for retiring professors, and a contribution to provide sneakers for the basketball team, money is never mentioned.

Last weekend was homecoming at McMaster University (which is my old college despite rumours you might hear, unfounded denials spread by faculty members). It was a moving occasion – walking through historic halls some of which date back to almost 1950, sitting in a windswept stadium where many of the great men of intercollegiate sport once played, invariably with visiting teams, looking into wave after wave of friendly faces and asking that great question of every reunion – "Who's that?"

It was particularly nostalgic because it was my birthday weekend, too. "I know why you're getting me out of the house," I said to my wife at the football game. "You're planning a surprise party. Right?"

"Aren't you always?" she said.

"Say, there's a girl I took out when I was at school . . ."

"My, she looks old," my wife said. "Here. Hold the baby."

"Why is it every time I see a girl I used to know you ask me to hold the baby?"

"Coincidence," she ensured.

Later we left the park (McMaster won 38-0 and my son beat my wife, three hot dogs to two).

"Everybody's hiding behind the furniture at home, eh? They'll jump out and say, 'Surprise!'"

"How did you guess?" my wife replied.

Well, there wasn't anyone at the house – just a birthday card from my insurance man who asks often how I'm feeling.

"Here's a package," my son advised.

It was a present from my mother-in-law, a book on Italian art, the very thing my wife has wanted for months.

"When's the party start?" I asked.

"Any minute now," my wife said.

"C'mon. Drop the act. I know you planned a surprise party."

"That's right," she said. "How about a quick supper – bacon and eggs?"

We ate silently.

My mother called. "I ordered a birthday cake," she said. "But there was a mixup. The one I've got says, 'Happy Birthday, Gary – aged two years.' It belongs to a lady out in the suburbs. We've got to deliver it and pick up yours."

"Okay," I said. "Anyway, happy birthday to me – aged thirty-five."

The evening went pretty fast. It was seven o'clock in no time. Then 7:15 and 7:30 and, finally, nearly quarter to eight.

"Guess I should stay dressed up," I suggested hopefully.

"Why not get comfortable," my wife said.

So I did. I can bluff, too.

It was getting pretty late. Almost 8:30. "We could catch a show downtown," I mentioned. "Should do something. Or would you rather stick around, just in case somebody drops in. Ha, ha." The laugh wasn't very convincing.

"A show would be fine," my wife said. "Should I get dressed?"

"Never mind. I'll just read." So I sat there.

"The babysitter tells me she thinks she's got chicken pox and wonders if she's given them to the kids," my wife mentioned.

"When I was single I always had a birthday party," I replied. "I got a cake, too. With candles."

"That's nice," she said.

"Here I am thirty-five and nobody cares."

"Your insurance man does."

"Oh, I think I'll go to bed."

"Why don't you? It's almost ten o'clock."

"Okay, I will."

Just then there was a knock on the door. About twenty-five people burst into the house and they said "Happy birthday." My wife brought out the lunch from down in the basement and I got one barbell, a genuine teakwood yo-yo, a bottle of Greasy Kid's Stuff, a jar of pickled pimentoes with a candle on the jar . . .

Somebody had an accordion and played polka music. The girls kissed me. (The baby was in bed so I didn't have to hold her.) My mother brought in the right cake and squeezed me and talked about the first night I was tucked under her arm — "I told the doctor I wanted a girl but I didn't care if it was pups just as long as he got it over with," she said.

"Were you surprised with the party?" my wife asked after the company had gone.

"Naw," I said. "I wasn't worried a bit."

"Did you get everything you wanted?"

"All the important things."

And we stood there, holding hands.

"Big mush," she said.

Romance on the sofa

Nothing is more embarrassing than being caught necking by your parents, especially if your mother is a Methodist. But that's what happened to me Sunday.

Let me make it clear that, ordinarily, I don't neck on Sunday. Sunday I cut the grass and watch football on TV. However, this Sunday I lost my head. The kids had gone to Sunday school and the house was quiet when I suggested to my wife, "Now that we're alone, why don't you slip into something more comfortable?"

"Like what?" she asked.

"Like the chesterfield, beside me," I responded.

"Aren't you going to cut the grass?" she wanted to know.

"Later," I snapped. "Come here!"

"Let me stack the breakfast dishes first," my wife replied.

"To heck with the breakfast dishes," I said, flaring my nostrils. "We've only got an hour."

I grabbed my wife by the hand and pulled her to the chesterfield where I proceeded to cover her forehead with kisses. The next thing I heard was somebody in the front hall.

"Anybody home?" a voice asked.

Yes – my mother.

My wife jumped up like a shot. Her hair was mussed and

the strap from her apron was down over one shoulder.

"I knocked but nobody answered," my mother explained as she came up the hall steps into the front room. My father was three steps behind. "The door was unlocked so . . ."

Then she spotted my wife trying desperately to rearrange her hair and adjust her apron straps.

"Oh," my mother said. "Oh!"

"I . . . I . . . I was just stacking the breakfast dishes," my wife blurted, slipping on her shoes.

Thinking quickly, I said, "Hi," looking mother straight in the shoulder. I never unflared a nostril so fast in my life.

They stayed for an hour, but it wasn't a relaxing visit. I knew that they knew what we were doing. And they knew that I knew that they knew what we were doing. But nothing was said.

However, I wish mother hadn't giggled as they backed out of the driveway to go home.

Lighting my wife's fire

It's a good thing I'm not a bachelor. I could never pass the physical. Just the other night I tried to light my wife's fire and the only thing that almost went up in flame was the house. Here's what happened.

I got home late, the kids were in bed — and I was feeling romantic. "Why don't you slip into something comfortable," I suggested to my wife, "and we'll have supper by the fireplace."

"What do you have in mind?" she queried.

"Oh, a little beef fondue, some candlelight, and a million kisses for dessert," I replied, sinking my teeth savagely into the shoulder strap of her apron and emitting a low animal groan.

"Okay," my wife agreed. "Get out the fondue burner and I'll be back in a few minutes."

"Every second will seem like an eternity," I vowed, bringing out the grade A material.

In ten minutes she reappeared wearing a backless jumpsuit, a hint of her best perfume, and a blue ribbon in her hair. She was also carrying a plate of chopped meat and a pot of cooking oil.

"She walks in beauty like . . ." I began.

"You'd better start the burner," my wife interrupted. "This is heavy."

"The heat from a thousand suns couldn't equal the flame that burns in this heart for you," I vowed. "It feeds on . . ."

"The burner?" my wife reminded.

"How do I love thee? Let me count the ways," I recited as I filled the burner and struck a match.

That's as far as I got. The whole damn table-top caught fire. With only candlelight to work by (and my glasses being upstairs) I had apparently poured too much fluid into the burner and it had overflowed. The only thing being shish-kabobed was the furniture.

"Stand back!" my wife shouted. She handed me the pot of cooking oil while she proceeded to beat the flames with a damp cloth from the kitchen.

Unfortunately, I got so excited I forgot about the cooking oil in my hand and tipped the pot while backing away from the fire scene. After my wife got the flames out, she noticed a peculiar gleam on the floor. Yes – cooking oil. And about a half inch deep, or so it seemed.

Using paper towelling, my wife got down on her hands and knees and began sopping up the oil, which had also splashed on the wall, the sewing machine, and my shoes. In about forty-five minutes, everything was more or less back to normal.

"My love's more richer than my tongue," I started up again.

"Knock it off while I get my wind back," she said, slumping in a chair.

Somehow I don't think seduction is my line of work.

Thin people are sexiest

Diet experts say thin people are sexy people. Well, take it from the soft voice of experience, they're right. Since Christmas I've lost nineteen pounds – I'm down to 163, my lowest since college. And, in the process, I've become a bottomless reservoir of passion. All I do in my spare time is smother my wife with tight-lipped kisses.

Take last night. We were watching television when a food commercial flashed on. It was for a gooey dessert. "Do they have to show this sort of thing on TV?" I demanded. "Don't they know I'm hungry enough to eat an end table?"

"Why don't you make yourself a snack?" my wife advised.

"You know I can't eat between meals!" I replied in astonishment. "I've already had as many calories as I'm allowed for the day."

"Then don't watch the commercial if it bothers you."

"How can I help but watch it? There it is right under my nose – a picture of banana cream pie covered with whipped cream and sprinkled with . . ." I ran up to the TV set and licked the screen.

"Why don't you drop over and visit Bill?" my wife suggested.

"Bill's wife is too good a cook. She'd offer me something and I might not be strong enough to refuse."

"Then go downtown."

"I can't. None of my clothes fit me since I lost the nineteen pounds," I grumbled.

"Why don't you get new clothes – or have the old ones taken in?" was the next question.

"Because I'm not sure I'll stay at 163. I don't want to spend a lot of money on clothes until my weight settles down."

"If you don't want to watch television, visit friends, or go downtown, what do you want to do?" my wife asked.

"Let's neck," I said.

"We necked last night," my wife reminded. "And the night before that. I've got ironing to do."

"I don't like necking any better than you," I told her, "but it keeps my mind off food."

And that's why people on diets are so sexy. In fact, if I stay on this diet much longer, I'm going to lose another 124 pounds. My wife says she'll leave me.

Sex secrets for sale

Like many others, ever since Shirley MacLaine made a bundle

for talking about her affairs, I've been trying to assess how much my personal sex secrets would be worth. So far, this is how I've got it figured out.

Item: on our first date, I distinctly remember driving my future wife home and saying in a low voice, "It's time to get down to some serious hand-holding." Which I did. Total value for any future sex book: thirty-eight cents.

Item: neither Jackie nor I can remember our first kiss but Mrs. Lautens says it took so long for me to make a move she was beginning to think there was something wrong with me. However, we think the kiss came on our third date and both agree we were wearing overcoats, snow boots, mufflers, gloves, etc., at the time. Bidding price for scandal purposes: seventy-five cents.

Item: goodnight kisses during the courtship were limited by several factors. One: as soon as we drove into the side drive, Jackie's mother always flicked the veranda lights on and off. In fact, for a time I thought Jackie lived in a lighthouse. Value of anecdote for sex excerpt: twenty-eight cents. Two: if we did get as far as the front hall, Jackie's mother regularly shouted down the stairs, "It's time Gary went home and you came to bed." Value to potential book publisher: fourteen cents. Three: Jackie's father weighed 220 pounds and enjoyed bending storm doors in two to indicate to his daughter's boy friends how he felt about hanky-panky. Market value for raunchy newspaper syndication: nineteen cents.

Item: we courted in a sports car, an MG, with the emergency brake in between the two seats, no heater, plastic windows that didn't fit, and it was the dead of winter. As a hot scene for possible film or TV series: four cents.

Item: during the entire romance, I had a runny nose, the unfortunate result of taking secret swimming lessons every morning at the YMCA so I wouldn't be unmasked to the blushing bride on the honeymoon (in Florida) as a non-swimmer who had to bob around on an inner tube while the light of his life was doing half-gainers from the highboard. I learned to swim in time but the sneezing put a definite crimp in the hugging and kissing department. Probable porno value on open market: nine cents.

Item: we got engaged in Buffalo, N.Y. Romantic value to world-wide distributor of literary rights: 0.

Item: when the subject of the honeymoon comes up, Jackie's favourite story concerns a police officer who stopped us on a Florida highway and was going to give us a ticket for speeding until he learned we were honeymooners. That was the highlight of the trip, Mrs. Lautens insists. Price TV station would pay for the explicit details: twenty-seven cents.

Item: the groom (me) still has the actual honeymoon pyjamas in the dresser drawer. A gift from his saucy bride, they are white and are covered with little red hearts and tiny owls that are saying, "Whoo do you love?" Value as a teasing chapter in a reveal-all volume: twenty-three cents.

Item: the only garter belt in the house is the one used by me years ago to keep up the hockey stockings in an industrial league. Possible bid from photographer interested in snapping the owner (still me) wearing same: two cents.

And that's it.

Believe me, when sex secrets are going for $1 million, it's pretty discouraging to think your own best stuff is worth only $2.39 (Canadian).

Putting the bite on romance

The old self-image is in tatters today. The spring has gone

from my step and I'd have to get some colour in my cheeks to pass as pale. I've just found out my kisses leave something to be desired. It's a crushing blow.

Over the years I've always considered myself pretty good at kissing. Maybe not Olympic gold but certainly above average. Let me put it this way: I've never had any serious complaints about my pecks, smacks, busses, etc. No lawyer's letter at least.

However, the other morning I learned that in the osculation profession I could be charged with carrying at least a semi-dangerous weapon. It seems this front tooth of mine (the one on the right) sticks out and can cause mischief if a person isn't careful.

How I found out was a little roundabout. I was talking to Mrs. Lautens about daughter Jane, who had braces on her teeth several years ago but is complaining her front teeth are getting out of line again.

"Jane thinks they should be re-straightened," Jackie informed me.

I pointed out that (a) Jane at seventeen has never had a cavity, (b) her teeth look fine to me, (c) the first orthodontic experience set Daddy back over $1,000.

"Besides," I said, "my front teeth are a little crooked and may be a teeny bucked, but they've never bothered anyone."

"Except me," Jackie blurted.

That's when the whole sordid story came out. Under direct questioning, Mrs. Lautens confessed the tooth I prize so much during the corn season, the one I use to peel oranges and snap off ketchup bottle caps, well, THAT tooth was not always a joy to the kissee.

"Unless a person knows what she's doing, she could bruise a lip pretty badly kissing you," the love of my life stated.

As the words fell, I could feel my fang creep back into the dark recesses of my mouth. Oh, the shame! Oh, the ignominy!

"Why did you wait twenty-three years before mentioning it?" I asked. "I could have kissed you on the other side of my mouth, the safe one."

Jackie indicated the tooth in question added a certain element of danger and excitement to our relationship but it certainly wasn't something she'd recommend for beginners like Jane. We decided to let the family dentist look at Jane's mouth and go along with his expert decision.

However, life has not been the same for me since the accidental disclosure of my dental shortcomings. Guilty memories have been flooding back. In my madcap youth did I innocently leave a trail of battered lips in the wake of my rogue tooth? Was this the real reason Norma didn't go out with me on second date, not because (as stated) she had a previous engagement in Bolivia? Did Elsie refuse to let me kiss her fingertips in that playful romp for fear I'd sever a major artery and end her career as catcher for the class softball team? Was I first pick at Hallowe'en parties for my ability to spear bobbing apples out of a tub rather than because of my personality? Are there dozens of women walking around at this very moment with highnecked dresses because of an impression I made on them years ago?

I suppose it's something I'll learn to live with. In the meantime, I'm not going to kiss anyone unless they can prove their OHIP is paid up, and they sign a release.

Report from the Lautens bed

I hate to bore you with a report on what happened in the Lautens bed the other day but it is on my mind. The planned article on the constitution will just have to wait.

Back to the bed.

If there's one thing Mrs. Lautens asks of life it's a cuddle.

The day must start with a cuddle and end the same way, or it has no meaning. This is Jackie's philosophy, and I couldn't agree more. When we turn in at night the first few minutes are always devoted to cuddling. Nothing torrid, mind you (after all, there may be children in the audience), but just a lovely comforting cuddle. Cuddle over, we then nod off, content that all is right with the world, or as right as it's apt to get in these mad times.

And when the clock-radio turns on in the morning, we have another cuddle before girding the loins and plunging into the day's hectic business. That is our habit and has been for twenty-three years past.

Naturally, as cuddle addicts, we have gone through some bleak moments, usually when we're away from home in a hotel that has only twin beds. Then, if the furniture isn't bolted down, I attempt to move the beds together so we won't be cruelly deprived of our daily dose of snuggling. The strain of moving a heavy Beautyrest with box spring puts even a sturdy back at risk, but it's worth it if you're hooked on cuddling.

On cool nights the physical advantages of cuddling are obvious; a warm back or leg is certainly better to curl up with than a book, even one by Mordecai or Gay.

The real advantages are mental and spiritual. When involved in a first-rate cuddle, it is impossible for a human being to harbour nasty thoughts, plan sleep-interrupting strategy for tomorrow's business meeting, replay the mistakes of the previous twelve hours, or develop a nervous hive over world events. At least that is how I've found it. When the missus and I cuddle at the end (or beginning) of the day, all I do is smile a lot.

Which brings me to a conversation Jackie and I had in bed the other morning. We were cuddling, about seventy zillion miles away from the rest of the world, when Jackie said: "You know, I hate sleeping alone. I think that's why I got married, so I'd have somebody to sleep with. Isn't cuddling great?"

"Mmmmm," was my answer.

"I still don't understand people who like twin beds," she continued. "It would be so lonely."

Why, I don't know, but a dark thought popped into my head and out of my mouth. "Nobody lives forever," I said. "When I'm dead and gone, what are you going to do for cuddles?"

Without the slightest pause, Jackie replied, "Who says I'm going to bury you?"

Then she cuddled closer.

You can see we take our cuddling seriously.

I'm pretty warm stuff in bed

I'd like to say Mrs. Lautens admires me for my mind, but what she really likes about me is my warm body. And, please, no tittering.

If I had a dollar for every time Jackie jumped into bed on a winter night, shivered up to me, and asked, "How come you're so warm?" I'd be having lunch today with Conrad Black instead of in the office caf.

To be straight about it, Jackie doesn't care that I use my fingers when adding numbers, or that I sometimes get my grammar wrong. As long as my body stays warm, she'll never leave me.

To the Resident Love Goddess I'm worth my weight in fifty-cents-off coupons. She wouldn't trade me for fifteen minutes' free shopping at Eddie Bauer, not in the weather we've been having lately. Jackie is always cold and will admit the only time from October to April she is goosebump-free is when she cuddles up to The Warm Body in bed.

I don't mind when she puts a cold foot on me, wraps a blue arm around my thermal shoulders, or uses my back as a toaster for some personal bit verging on frostbite. Like Old Faithful, I am only too happy to do missionary work among the teeth-chattering and share my warm. In fact, I'm rather humbled to see the circulation and colour gradually return to Jackie's nose and cheeks.

Within a few minutes Mrs. Lautens is cosy and warm, and nodding off, undoubtedly to dream about walking in the hot sand of some tropic island, or stretching out on the most expensive deck of a cruise ship in the Caribbean.

Why I was chosen by some Unseen Hand to be the possessor of a warm body, I don't know. It's a mystery which, perhaps, no human dare explore. The plain fact is I have a warm body, just as some people have thick mops of hair, a baby toe that bends under, or the ability to wiggle their ears. Cold doesn't bother me.

Having a warm body is a responsibility, of course, and not one I take lightly. I'd never exploit my warm body or use it except for the betterment of mankind. For example, no matter what kind of marital spat Jackie and I might have had, I'd never threaten to take my warm body away, even though it would mean her immediate capitulation and victory for me, especially if there's frost on the windows.

When the thermostat for the evening is down to 55, and the wind's howling, I know I have an unfair advantage. It would be cruel to resort to the ultimate weapon on a person who, without your warm body, could be a human icicle in a matter of minutes.

No, my motto is: no argument is worth winning at the risk of another person's life, or chilblains.

How many others in the nation have been blessed with

warm bodies, I don't know. But I do know it's our duty to make sure the less fortunate come through February, and without turning into popsicles or momsicles in the process. My only regret is that I have but one warm back to give to the missus. Still, it gets her through the night.

Aquatic Adventures

How a kiss turned Prince Gary into a frog

Men do all sorts of things for the love of a woman. Edward the Eighth gave up his throne for the woman he loved. Macbeth gave up his peace for the woman he loved. Romeo gave up his family – and life – for the woman he loved.

But I gave up my rubber duck for mine. And greater love hath no man than that. Rubber ducks, as you may realize, don't grow on trees.

But it was more than that. My rubber duck represented security. It comforted me in troubled waters. It was like a beacon to me. More important, it kept me from drowning whenever I was in water deeper than my nose.

You see, when I met Jackie, I was a confirmed non-swimmer. Oh, I had dabbled here, waded there. But swimming wasn't my cup of tea. Some people look at water and see beauty, mystery, and challenge. My reaction to water for the first twenty-eight years of my life could be summed up in two words: "Glub, glub." I hated water.

But there I was, going out with this blonde girl who had been raised on a beach, a girl who had water on the knee and everywhere else for the first eighteen years of her life. She considered Esther Williams a landlubber.

Anyway, when we began talking about marriage and honeymoons, Jackie mentioned she would like to go to Florida for a vacation.

Well, as it happened, most of our courting was done during the winter months and Jackie didn't know that the only thing I could do in the water was play dead – and very effectively.

Male pride what it is, I had two choices: I could either throw Jackie back and bait my hook for something that didn't go

splash. Or, I could learn to swim.

The choice wasn't easy but I finally decided if anybody was going to give me mouth-to-mouth resuscitation, it was going to be Jackie.

So I started to take lessons. Every day through the dead of winter I'd go over to the YMCA and practise sinking. And I got to be very good at it. With very little practice, I was soon able to duck my head under water, to open my eyes under water, and even hold my breath under water. It wasn't until about the tenth lesson that I figured out the whole trick of swimming was to stay *above* water. As I recall, a lot more than my pride was swallowed those months. I had enough chlorine in me to open my own pumping station.

But after weeks and weeks of pretending the water was my friend (I knew darn well that the water hated me and was just waiting for a chance to swallow me whole) I finally managed enough of the dog paddle to feel qualified to make the trip up the aisle.

In case you're wondering, I didn't exactly dazzle my bride on the honeymoon with my aquatic skills but I was at least able to go wading without the services of my rubber duck. Nothing ruins the heroic image of a man faster than a lot of bubbles coming from his nose at the bottom of the ocean. It puts an awful crimp in the honeymoon, too.

After we got settled into the routine of marriage, swimming wasn't very high on our list of things to do. In fact, as far as I was concerned, it came right after flying to the moon and learning how to play the musical saw. For almost ten years I was able to keep up the little game. I wouldn't even watch Lloyd Bridges on television. That's how far away from water I kept.

However, three summers ago I got hooked into buying this home with a swimming pool as part of the deal. My wife couldn't have been happier if I tossed her a fish. So, at age thirty-seven, I had to start all over again – kick, gasp, kick, gasp, kick.

All the kids can swim now like their mother. They do the crawl, the breaststroke, the butterfly.

And me? Would you believe I was once a handsome prince until along came this pretty girl who kissed me and turned me into a frog?

Croak! Croak!

The amazing Lautens spa

I am certain that long lines of pilgrims will soon be forming in front of my home and that the name Lautens will one day rank with Pasteur, Banting, and Salk in the medical texts. Or, perhaps, I may put Lourdes or the Ganges right out of business as pilgrimage spots. That is, if the police don't nab me first for practising medicine without a license. You see, I'm operating a clinic.

It wasn't supposed to be a clinic. It was supposed to be a swimming pool. But it didn't work out that way. I was always under the impression that a swimming pool was filled with water. Fortunately, I found out better. A swimming pool is filled with chemicals. Chemicals to kill germs. Chemicals to kill algae. Chemicals to kill fungus, rot, and blight of every description.

Up until now, I've only used chlorine and muriatic acid, shaking in enough every day to keep my backyard bathtub kissing sweet. No bad breath for this Flipper. However, the good man who supplies my pool needs has convinced me I've only been half-safe. He's just sold me a third chemical which, when added to the other chemicals, even prevents and treats athlete's foot. He says you can now eat off my pool, it's so clean.

My pool bubbles. It gleams. A mouse fell into it the other day and was dead before it hit bottom. Now that's what I call antiseptic.

I'm sure you could bathe in my spa and be cured of boils, sprains, toothache, fallen arches, and that curious rash you have on your stomach. Undoubtedly crutches and eye glasses will soon be heaped beside my diving board, silent tributes to the miracles wrought by modern science and the dog paddle. After a refreshing dip, I myself notice a tingle in my muscles. The silver fillings in my teeth are left glistening. And I have a general feeling of well-being.

Each day I go out and feed my pool, tossing in chemicals by the handful and listening to the little bacilli go "Ugh!" as they keel over in a death rattle. I'm so pleased I may even have a particularly splendid cocci I bagged just last week stuffed and mounted for the fireplace.

To make sure I get the right mixture (one pail of water for every 35,000 gallons of chemicals) I even have a testing kit and, so far, my pool is in perfect balance.

Only one thing worries me. The more I swim, the shorter I get. Do you think you could learn to love a man who is two feet, three inches tall and hasn't got athlete's foot?

How to kill a swimming pool

Usually our swimming pool doesn't turn green until the middle of July. Once it didn't die until almost September. But this year we established a new record. Our water developed terminal algae by the first week in June. It turned up its toes before we had a chance to dunk ours. We didn't need a lifeguard in the backyard. We needed a medic who could treat swamp fever.

How did we manage it? Frankly, I was baffled too. It was more than strange; it was Erie. Naturally, I called George. George is the man who takes care of two things – my swimming pool and my savings. George can't understand why I complain about my salary. He can get along on it very nicely.

"George," I reported, "the pool has turned green."

"Are you putting in chlorine?" he wanted to know.

"Of course," I told him.

"Double the dose," George instructed, "and call me in the morning."

I did as he said but by morning the pool still looked like a subdivision for frogs.

"This calls for drastic action," George agreed. "You'd better super-chlorinate. Throw in four times the usual amount."

I did. Nothing.

"Have you tested the pool?" George asked when informed of the lack of results.

"Yes," I said, "and I don't get any reading."

George confessed he was stymied.

"Could the chlorine lose its potency over the winter?" I suggested. "It's been in the garage since last September."

"I never heard of it happening," he replied. "Maybe I'd better come over and take a look at your water."

"Yes – and bring $38.95," I stated. "I want a refund on that chlorine you sold me. It's no damn good." Then I hung up.

Later in the day I was working in the garage, getting the de-humidifier set up for summer. And I couldn't find the calcium stuff that goes in it to absorb moisture. Pow! It hit me. Last winter I needed a place to keep the calcium – so I used an empty chlorine pail. What I'd been dumping in the pool was . . .

Well, our water may be green, but it's very dry. I'd better call George.

Midnight swimmers

I'd like to explain about the party you saw at my house the other evening. I know. It looked bad. You can't have seven lovely girls in bikinis running around the backyard at midnight without starting a few rumours, I suppose. But I'm innocent. So help me, it wasn't my idea.

I give you my word this is how it happened. My wife and I were watching the eleven o'clock news on television when there was a knock on the front door. When I answered it, there were these seven girls – hardly more than children, really – standing in the doorway. They were wearing short coats as far as I could make out because an awful lot of leg was showing. I admit that. Anyway, one of the girls spoke right up: "Mister," she said, "could we go swimming in your pool?"

What was a fellow to say? You can't turn away seven needy girls from your swimming pool, especially at eleven o'clock at night. Naturally, I agreed.

I asked them if they had a place to change and they said that wasn't necessary. They whipped off their coats, and they were standing in their bikinis before I could say, "Golly willickers!"

Don't ask me how they arrived at my doorstep. Maybe they go door-to-door every evening looking for a place to swim. All I know is that I had never laid eyes on them before.

When I got back in the house my wife asked who was at the door and I explained how these little tykes had asked to go swimming.

"That's nice," she agreed. Then she took a look at them herself from the back window.

"Tykes!" she exclaimed. "They're sixteen or seventeen if they're a day."

I told her I didn't get a good look at them and that she might very well be right.

Anyway, there I was with a pool full of young girls, splashing and diving, giggling and showing their form on the diving board. Naturally, I can only guess at what they were doing. Other than checking the chlorine level of the pool, turning on the lights, asking them if the temperature was just right, handing them towels, taking them soft drinks, and making sure they were good swimmers, I didn't go into the backyard once.

My wife was nice about it, too, once she understood. In fact, she didn't say another word the rest of the evening.

Shortly after midnight I had to go out to tell the girls that I was going to bed and that they had better take one last splash before the lights went out.

They did.

Maybe that's what woke you up – all the laughter and noise.

They dried themselves off, thanked me over and over, and then walked off down the street in their bikinis, their coats hanging from their shoulders.

And that's all there is to it. I swear.

Naturally, I invited the girls back any time they're passing. It makes you feel warm inside when you can help a fellow human being like that. Besides, seven is my lucky number.

Mother, will you come out to swim?

Why does a man slave to put in a swimming pool? Is it for his children? Is it to avoid the headache of driving north weekends to some faraway cabin to escape city heat? Is it for investment purposes, or prestige? Of course he says it's all those things.

But the real reason we men put in backyard swimming pools is because we think we'll get a chance to skinny-dip with the wife. No use denying it. As we sign the contract with Foamy Pools Ltd., we can picture ourselves cavorting starkers with the missus in a spanking new 40-by-20, playing like baby seals in the moonlight while the rest of the world sleeps, or whatever.

Now isn't that a lovely thought!

Well, you've hardly had time to turn on the taps, and send the cheque to Foamy Pools, before you learn your wife has no intention of joining you in your midnight swim. Especially without a stitch.

You can make all sorts of pretty speeches about the joy of swimming *au naturel*, the thrill of doing the Australian crawl or even backstroke with nothing between you and the sky but stars, the freedom of taking the plunge without something by Speedo or Jantzen tugging every-which-way.

You can say all those things. You can even promise not to snap your towel at her.

No matter.

Wives want no part of a skinny dip. Daddy can do whatever he wants; she'll stay inside, buttoned, hooked, and zipped up.

In the eight years we've had a swimming pool, my wife has turned down suggestions of a midnight skinny dip on the grounds that it's too cold, it's too warm, it's too dark, it's too late, it's too close after dinner. She has complained about

having a headache, not knowing where her beach towel is, and that she was expecting a phone call.

She has also said she didn't want to miss Johnny Carson (who evidently was having a particularly good show that night), that Richard had a little fever and might want a glass of water at any moment, that the neighbours seven doors down were having a party and might see, and that the street-light across the road was giving off too much light.

Once, so help me, she said she couldn't go skinny-dipping at 11:30 at night because she had ironing to do.

At a rough guess I'd say I've suggested a skinny dip to Jackie 800 times, and 800 times I've been unsuccessful.

So (you're asking yourself) why don't I give up, get rid of the pool, and forget about skinny dips? Simple. Whenever Jackie turns down my invitations to a little midnight swim, she always finishes with the same phrase, "Maybe tomorrow night."

Well, it isn't a definite "no."

Broken Legs and House Husbandry

On becoming a ski racer

For thirty-nine years I've been able to go through life with one proud boast on my lips: No. I don't ski. It's been a major accomplishment. I could fail ink-blot tests, fit square pegs in round holes, climb the TV antenna and bay at the moon – but not a hospital in the world would ever commit me, not when they found out I was smart enough not to take up skiing.

Well, I've fallen. Don't ask me why. Maybe my father dropped me when I was a baby. Perhaps I nurtured a secret desire to wear plaster and have people write funny things on my hips. But there I was, agreeing to fall down some mountain I hardly knew – and pay for the privilege. I couldn't believe my dumb lips. Why should I take up skiing? I don't even like hot buttered rum.

Anyway, the first job was to put on the ski clothes which, to put it mildly, fit rather tight. In fact, when I put on the ski pants, I felt like a loaded slingshot. If my braces ever slipped off my shouders, I knew I'd be accordioned to death. Then came the wool shirt, the sweaters, a thick hat, a heavy jacket, a scarf, goggles, boots, and two pairs of mitts.

My friends asked me if I could move and, when I assured them I couldn't, they pronounced me ready to go skiing. They carried me to the beginner's hill (designed for small children, expectant mothers, and sissies) and I got my first lesson in self-destruction. Skiing, I've learned, is to North Americans what kerosene is to Buddhist monks.

The instructor, a fellow named Ron Sadist, spent the first thirty minutes telling me the best way to enjoy skiing. He told me, for example, that skiing is more fun if you don't run into tree stumps at 40 mph. He also said there were limited laughs in sailing over cliffs and holding onto the tow rope too long. He told me how to fall down, how to get up, how to slip out of skis in an emergency, and what to do while waiting for the ski patrol to pick me up in a toboggan.

"What do you do when your hands get cold?" I asked.

"You jump up and down and say, 'Isn't this fun! Isn't this fun!'" he explained.

I tried it but it kept coming out, "I must be nuts. I must be nuts."

Finally I was ready to be launched. "I hope I don't break anything," I said to him.

"If you break anything, make sure it's a leg," he warned. "Everything else is rented."

Down I went. I skidded. I slid. I did something called a snowplow. I also sagged. But I got clear down to the bottom without sitting down.

Triumph!

On the tow going back up the hill, I said to Ron: "How much would it cost me for boots, harness, and, maybe, racing skis?"

A glorious ski weekend

I was bitten by the ski bug about a month ago so you can imagine how excited I was when I got a chance to borrow a friend's cottage in the mountains last weekend.

"Boy, oh boy! Are we going to have fun!" I announced to my wife when I got home with the good news.

My wife never answered. It's amazing how she can conceal her enthusiasm even at moments like these.

"We'll pack the kids, drive 475 miles, and be skiing that very day," I enthused. "I'll arrange everything."

All we needed was skis, boots, harness, poles, goggles, wax, waterproofing, sweaters, parkas, mitts, apres-ski ensembles, and a rack to carry everything on the car roof. In the past, I always rented. This time I bought the works. It cost a bundle but when you're going to have that kind of fun, who worries about money?

The day we left home, it was pouring rain. "Boy, oh boy! Are we going to have fun?" I repeated gamely. "I can't wait to get to the mountains and see all that snow."

My wife just gave me a friendly glare and told the kids to stop fighting in the back seat, or she'd throw them out the window at 60 mph. (She's great with that child psychology stuff.)

When we got to the mountains, it was still raining. "Never mind," I said. "It's going to turn to snow overnight and we'll ski tomorrow." The next morning it was still raining.

"We'll get our boots adjusted, wax the skis, and check our gear until the snow starts to fall this afternoon," I suggested bravely. "And then – zoom! Are we going to have . . ."

"I know – fun," my wife interrupted. And then she ran off to stop the children from feeding the baby – to the animals outside.

I have to admit even I was getting discouraged. It rained when we went to town for supplies. It rained during dinner. It rained that evening. And we were down to our last day.

"It's almost thirty-two degrees," I pointed out as we went to bed. "Just another degree or two and we'll be sliding . . ."

My wife was already asleep so I never finished my Knute Rockne speech.

When we woke up in the morning, there it was – snow, glorious snow! And the hills were only a twenty-minute drive away!

"Get dressed," I ordered. "We'll be the first ones on the tow. Boy, oh boy! Are we going to have fun?"

"Think so?" my wife replied, pointing to the road. Or where it was supposed to be. We were snow-bound.

The ploughs came past at four o'clock that afternoon – just in time for us to get a really good look at the ski hills on the way home.

Now I'm lady of the house

I'm the kind of guy who worries when his wife goes out for an afternoon of fun and comes home with her underwear tucked under her arm. I know it's silly but that's how I am. So you can imagine how my forehead wrinkled the other day when Jackie opened the front door.

There she was, exactly as when she left – but with her underwear in a neat roll under one arm and a friend (female) under the other.

"Hi," Jackie said.

"I thought you were skiing," I responded.

"I was," she agreed.

Just then part of her underwear fell out of her grasp and landed on the floor.

"Have a good time?" I asked.

"No . . . not exactly . . ."

"Jackie had a little accident," her friend interrupted. "We had to take her to the hospital for x-rays and, well, Jackie can tell you the rest. Good-bye."

Exit, one friend.

"What happened?" I asked when we were alone.

"I was taking just one more run before coming home and I went down the smallest hill and I hit some deep snow and I fell and they had to call the ski patrol and they brought me down the hill on a toboggan and they took me to the hospital and the doctor thinks I have a hairline fracture in my knee and I feel just awful," she said.

"Thank God!" I said. "For a minute I thought it was serious."

"It is serious," my wife blubbered.

"Not as serious as I thought it was," I told her. "By the way, your underwear is dragging on the ground."

"Those are my long johns," she explained. "After the x-rays, I couldn't get them on again.

With a little help from me, Jackie limped to bed – and that's where she is right now. She's got her leg propped in the air and her après-ski outfit consists of flannelette pyjamas and a plaster cast from her thigh to her ankle. If I didn't know better, I'd swear I was married to Angelo Mosca or Whipper Watson.

I'm in charge of the house so it's my job to help the kids get dressed, prepare breakfast, do the dishes, sweep up, go to the office, get home early, make (or buy) supper, answer telephone calls from people wanting to know how Jackie is, get the kids to bed, do a little dusting, etc. And then, at night, I sleep on a spare cot so that Jackie's knee won't be jiggled while it heals.

Today I had an uncontrollable urge to get Jackie's skis and throw the rotten things out on the front lawn in a gesture of defiance.

Revenge!

But then I remembered how much they cost and discarded my plan. Everything has a price apparently, even my right-eousness.

A lesson on using a refrigerator

It's taken forty-one years but I'm finally getting the real lowdown on how to run a kitchen. Every evening my wife props up her broken leg on a kitchen chair and gives me instructions on how to prepare dinner, what pots to use, which button on the stove to press, etc. Last night's lesson was on the use of the refrigerator.

I was cleaning up when my wife asked, "What are you doing now?"

"I'm taking the mashed potatoes we didn't finish at dinner and putting them in the garbage," I answered.

"Wrong," my wife chided. "You don't throw out mashed potatoes like that."

"What do I do with them?"

"You get a plastic baggie out of the top drawer and put the mashed potatoes inside of it."

"Then what?"

"You put the mashed potatoes in the refrigerator. They'll keep."

"There's only a spoonful or two left," I protested.

"When you're running a kitchen, you've got to learn not to throw out perfectly good food," my wife advised.

"But . . ."

"Don't argue – just put the mashed potatoes in the refrigerator."

"All right," I surrendered.

It took a couple of minutes but I scraped the mashed potatoes into the bag and prepared to put it away.

"Very good," my wife encouraged. "Now, while the refrigerator door is open, see if you can reach the plastic bag at the back of the middle shelf."

I said I could.

"Throw it in the garbage," came my next order.

"What's in it?" I asked.

"Mashed potatoes."

"Let me get this straight," I pleaded. "Do you want me to put mashed potatoes in the refrigerator, or to throw them out?"

"Both," she said.

"If you've already got cold mashed potatoes in the refrigerator, why don't you just let me throw out the ones left over from tonight's dinner?" I suggested.

"Because tonight's leftover potatoes are fresher than the leftover potatoes I've already got in the refrigerator."

"Then when will you throw out tonight's leftover mashed potatoes?"

"Probably next week," my wife admitted.

"We never eat leftover mashed potatoes at any time," I pointed out. "Why do you bother wrapping them up and putting them in the refrigerator?"

"Because I hate waste," my wife explained. "By the way, don't throw out that gravy. Get some plastic wrap and a jar and . . ."

Wife's crutches an added weapon

I thought my chances of finally winning a domestic scrap (after thirteen years of marriage) would be immeasurably

improved after my wife broke her leg skiing. After all, how tough can a 124-pound blonde be, especially if she has to hop on one leg to catch you?

The answer is plenty.

As it turns out, the accident has added just one more weapon to my wife's arsenal of tricks. You'd better make that two weapons – both crutches.

Not only do the crutches keep her up, they keep the rest of us down. The other day, for example, the kids were tearing through the house just slightly faster than the speed of sound. Now, ordinarily, you have to wait until they tire a bit – and then tackle them before they get their second wind. Not any more. My wife just sat calmly on the chesterfield – and stuck out a crutch when the little tykes made the turn into the kitchen a good six feet away.

Pow! They were down like bowling pins.

"Stop running," my wife ordered, wiggling the rubber tip of her crutch under their noses.

The rest of the morning they were very subdued. Wouldn't you be if you had a mother with a twelve-foot arm span?

Nobody or nothing is safe any more. We were in the family room the other evening when my wife spotted a spider crawling on the ceiling. Zap! She crutched him to death without getting out of her chair. The poor little fellow didn't know what hit him.

Thanks to her crutches, my wife is sort of a Hardwood Pimpernel. She's here, she's there, she's everywhere. Believe me, it's dangerous being married to The Fastest Crutch In The East. Just yesterday my wife and I were discussing something and, since I'm the more mobile at the moment, I was confident I'd get the last word in.

" . . . and that's final," I suggested, turning to make my exit.

"I'm not through yet," my wife said. And she plunked her crutch down on my foot.

I couldn't move. Only after she got in her say did my wife lift the crutch and finally release me. It sure put a dent in my ego.

However, I've got an ace up my sleeve. Some night when my wife's not looking I'm going to infect her crutches with Dutch elm disease. Let her explain that to the health department.

The stumbling gourmet

My wife's knee and I have two things in common: we're the sole support of my wife. And we're both sore at this moment. But there the comparison ends.

For example, the knee has been getting nothing but rest since Jackie had a skiing accident. On the other hand, I haven't sat down once since she took a spill and landed on her two most sensitive points – her pride and her kneecap.

The doctor claims the injury isn't serious – just a slight fracture. However, I can't say the same for me. Thanks to that knee, I'm bushed, bothered, and beleaguered. Everything has given out, including my temper.

To be perfectly frank, I'm not crazy about Jackie sliding down mountains on a pair of expensive fibre-glass runners in the first place. If I had wanted to marry Jean Claude Killy, I'd have asked him. What I wanted was somebody who was soft, cuddly, and a good cook. Unfortunately, at the moment, what I've got is a partner who, with her leg wrapped up in plaster and an elastic bandage, looks like a cross between a Canadian and an Egyptian mummy.

What does that mean to me? For one thing, from failing hands I've been thrown not a torch but an apron. I'm in charge of putting enough grub inside my kids so that they won't keel over at recess with malnutrition and cause a big scandal.

Alas! This is one gourmet who doesn't gallop. Stumble might be the better word. If James Beard ever saw what I do with food he'd probably lay a charge of assault and battery – or arson. I can get by breakfast all right. Cornflakes, toast, orange juice, and a vitamin pill each. Ditto lunch. How much talent does it take to make a peanut butter sandwich that will glue a kid's mouth shut so he can't ask for dessert?

But supper is my Achilles heel. Isobel has sent over some tidbits. So have my mother, Pat-down-the-street, and Carlo (who runs a takeout pizza place). My trouble is I can never get things ready in the proper order. For example, Isobel's chocolate pudding was just at the right temperature before the roast my mother left me was cooked.

What do you do in a case like that? We ate chocolate pudding as an appetizer and then dug into the meat course, forgetting completely about the vegetables, which weren't done until about eight o'clock that evening. It was like putting on your underwear after you've pulled on your trousers – but, when you're hungry, who cares?

Well, the kids for one.

They don't seem to have an appetite for roast beef after they've polished off a couple of bowls of chocolate pudding. They said the gravy tasted like Hershey bars. I couldn't even tempt them with a late snack of boiled potatoes and beets served up just before they went to bed.

Happily, I've discovered that youngsters love peanuts, which are a snap to prepare, if you can find the red tab on the cellophane package. I don't think serving them three times a day, and between meals, is too much although I do find it strange that Stephen has this curious desire now to hang upside down from the light fixtures. At least he's out of the way.

My other complaint about this skiing injury concerns the sleeping arrangements at our house. Ordinarily, my wife and

I share a double bed which, on cold winter nights, has certain advantages. However, because of the sore knee, which hurts even when viewed from closer than ten feet, my wife has taken over the bed completely. After making meals, writing columns, cleaning up, and issuing bulletins to friends on the state of my wife's knee, I'm relegated to the spare bedroom, where the only thing I can wrap myself up in is the cobwebs.

These are dark days for me – and the nights are no fun either.

The joy of charity

Thanks to my wife's broken leg, we have a new standard of living at our house. You'll think I'm gloating but, at this very moment, we have a huge lasagna in the refrigerator, a pan of stuffed steaks waiting only to be heated – and a casserole brimming with mysterious goodies. We also have a lemon chiffon cake, some chocolate chip cookies, two quarts of vanilla cherry ice cream, and a strawberry pie. And that's just today's take.

As it's turned out, the best break I've had in years is the one just below my wife's kneecap in her left leg. I didn't catch on to my good fortune right away. In fact, the first few days after the ski accident were grim, as I may have mentioned.

But then the plaster cast began to pay dividends. First Isobel (who lives around the corner) came over with a dish of spaghetti and her homemade sauce, which I can only describe as the best thing to come out of Italy since pinching.

"I hope you won't feel insulted if I bring over something for you and the children to eat," she apologized, "but I know it must be difficult for Jackie to get around the kitchen."

I assured Isobel that she wouldn't hurt my feelings if she brought over spaghetti (and her homemade sauce) from now till doomsday.

Although I didn't realize it, that was the turning point in my career as a homemaker. As soon as word got around that Jackie was laid up and that I wasn't too proud to accept charity, the food began to pour in. And not just *any* food.

Because they realized their donation to our supper table was being compared with recipes whipped up by others on the street, the neighbours began to outdo each other. Patricia delivered a steaming plate of filet done in some wine sauce that was strictly topflight. Marion turned out several dreamy desserts. Doreen came over one day with a complete dinner on a huge tray, everything from salad to barbecued chicken to homemade rolls to blueberry cheesecake – and she set our table as a bonus.

That's how it's gone day after day. Why, just yesterday, honest, we had *three* main courses brought around to the house.

So now you know why my refrigerator is groaning under the load.

Unfortunately, there is a price to pay for all this high living. Every husband in the district glares at me when I go past – and I can't blame them. I've been in the same boat. I've watched my wife turn out gourmet meals for somebody down the street and then been forced to settle for hash myself because she's too pooped to prepare anything better for her own.

But now that I'm on the receiving end of all this kindness, not to mention calories, I'm not going to knock it. When the ladies bring over bowls heaped high with mouth-watering treats, a small tear forms in my eye (I can make either eye glisten in gratitude now) and I say, "Bless you." Or, on occasion, I murmur, "Oh, you shouldn't have!" I am careful to say

this, however, without conviction. If someone like Isobel asks
how my wife's feeling, I sadly reply, "About as well as can be
expected, I suppose."

And, after the door is closed and Isobel's gone, I shout,
"Soup's on, gang!" And we all race for the dinner table,
Jackie included. Jackie is usually first to the kitchen because
she (unfairly, I think) uses her crutches to trip the rest of us
and hamper our movement.

So you can see what the broken leg means to our stomachs.
It's our meal ticket. We are living like kings – and it's costing
me only about $6 a week for milk, sugar, ketchup, etc., little
items the neighbours (up till now) have neglected to bring.

I don't care what the doctor says. I'm keeping Jackie's leg in
a cast till Christmas at least. Why heal a good thing?

A beginner's guide to supermarkets

While my wife is on crutches with her broken leg, I've been
doing the family shopping and these are some of the things
I've learned about supermarkets:

Shopping carts all have one defective wheel which makes
them impossible to steer straight.

Today's "specials" include dented cans of boiled turnip,
parts of the cow you never knew it had, and a brand of ketchup
your kids won't eat on a bet.

Before you get the chicken checked through, it leaks all over
your groceries and down the front of your trousers, causing all
sorts of nasty stories to start.

It's possible to get whiplash if rear-ended by a four-year-old pushing his mother's shopping cart.

There is no dignified way for a woman in a skirt to lean over the milk bin and pick up a three-quart jug of 2 per cent.

When shopping for a family of five, it's only possible to get pork chops in packages of four.

Large bags of potatoes are invariably on the supermarket floor and can be lifted with safety into your cart only if you have won a medal at a recent weight-lifting competition of international standard, have at least one teen-aged son with you to take the other end, or are wearing a truss or some other recognized support.

The roast in the next person's shopping cart looks better.

Supermarkets place their frozen foods at the most distant point in the store so that by the time you get to the checkout counter you can see it melting at the corners or hear it swishing in the can.

At the fruit counter, there is one rule: if you can reach it, don't take it. (A veteran shopper wouldn't consider taking home a grapefruit unless he or she dug it out from the bottom of the display, and had to get a boost to grasp it.)

Every supermarket has at least one aisle where someone has dropped a bottle (economy size) of salad dressing.

The most friendly clerks in the supermarket are in the fruit section while the most abrupt tend to be in the meat division, possibly because the first words expressed by most customers when they look at the price tag on a package of steaks is, "They've got to be kidding."

Novice shoppers can be spotted trying to figure out whether it's better to buy a five-pound box of washday miracle for $2.07 and get a bonus towel, another brand not advertised on TV but only $1.65 with a china figurine inside, or let the entire family go dirty for the week.

In the express line-up for eight-items-or-less, there's always a shopper with 18 items, plus a plant.

All checkout girls are named Helen, have a plastic flower

on their smock, and ask, "Do you have two pennies?"

Finally, I've learned one thing going to the supermarket: I'm getting stronger every year. Why, five years ago I could barely manage to lift $35 worth of groceries, and now I can carry $70 worth with ease.

Her broken leg is just a crutch

My wife's been on crutches for over five weeks and, as you can imagine, the house is beginning to look a little tacky. Our dog spilled some dinner yesterday and, when she tried to lap it up, her tongue stuck to the kitchen floor; and the kids at this minute are building a tree-house in the cobwebs in one corner of the living room. I think you'll agree that's tacky.

Whenever I bring up the subject of housework, however, Jackie always points to her crutches and claims they make work impossible. She is really taking her broken leg seriously.

Finally, I decided to have a talk. "Instead of thinking of your crutches as a handicap, you should regard them as a wonderful advantage," I began. "For example, there's no reason you couldn't put a scouring pad on the end of a crutch and clean out the corners of an oven normally out of reach. And the same goes for the dusting. Why, I bet you could stand in the middle of the room and do all the furniture, even the picture frames, without moving an inch.

"Crutches are a wonderful asset for a homemaker," I continued. "You can flip on the vacuum without all that nasty bending over. You can tuck in a bedspread without racing from side to side. You can hang damp towels on a crutch to dry. We'll take a chance that they won't warp."

Jackie didn't say a word.

"Housework would be fun on crutches," I bubbled. "Imagine trying to fold laundry with a pair of crutches. Gosh, that would be a riot. It would keep you amused for hours.

"You're really lucky. You can beat everyone to the phone by at least five feet. You can clear the dinner table with one fell swoop. You can pick up after the kids from the next room.

"Mind you, I don't think you should shovel snow yet on your crutches, or lift really heavy baskets of wash. But it would give you something to do if we put buffing pads on your crutches and let you shuffle through the downstairs, waxing the floors, or would you rather start in the boys' bathroom? I walked in there yesterday and the odor-eaters in my shoes died. Or we could hammer a nail in the crutches and, when you're not taking therapy, you could pick up the newspapers that get left on the living . . ."

At that moment Jackie took a swing at me with one of her crutches, but I ducked in time. Women with broken legs certainly lose their sense of humour, don't they?

Our house will stay tacky until further notice.

Housework and a passionate wife

There's been an amazing change in me since my wife broke her leg and I took over the housework. Just the other day, for example, Jackie came home from her daily therapy session and started across the front hall on her crutches.

"Did you wipe your foot?" I demanded. "I've just waxed that hall and I don't want it tracked up."

"I think my foot's clean," she responded.

"Thinking isn't good enough," I admonished. "I'm not getting down on my hands and knees and scrubbing a floor just for the good of my health. Take your shoe off."

Jackie slipped out of her loafer.

"You'll never believe what those kids did while you were away," I said.

"Couldn't it wait till later?" my wife begged. "I've had a tough day downtown and the traffic was murder."

"No, it couldn't," I answered. "I want you to give Richard a licking. He's been a little brat all afternoon."

"What did he do?"

"What didn't he do would be a better question. He put his knee through his pants playing football on the lawn, he punched his sister, he . . ."

"Calm down," my wife said. "Don't get so excited."

"You'd be excited, too, if you had to spend all day with these children," I said, bursting into tears. "They don't appreciate anything I do. I made them a beautiful lunch – peanut butter and honey sandwiches – and they hardly ate a bite. You don't know what it's like to slave in that kitchen and then have them turn up their noses at my meals," I sobbed.

"There, there," my wife comforted. "I'll speak to Richard later."

"You're no better," I complained. "I've been dusting and cleaning in the front room most of the afternoon but do you notice? Of course not. You're taking me for granted. It's okay for you to be downtown, taking therapy, but I've got to keep this house clean, feed the children, and then try to look nice when you come home. Frankly, I'm fed up. I'm fed up with housework. I'm fed up with picking up after people. I'm fed up with dirty dishes and folding the laundry and planning meals. For two cents I'd chuck it all and go home to mother."

"Why don't we just sit down and have a little quiet time to ourselves?" my wife suggested.

"All right – but hang your coat up first," I ordered.

"Can I put my arm around you?" my wife asked.

"No."

"Why not?"

"Because you think sex is the answer to everything," I told her. "And take your hand off my knee."

"Come on. How about a little kiss?"

"I'm **not** in the mood," I said. "Besides, I've got a headache."

"A little kiss will make you feel better," was her reply.

"The children may walk in," I warned. "How would it look if they found us like that?"

"They're playing around the corner," my wife stated. "I saw them when I came home."

"I think I'd better get supper started," I announced.

"It can wait," my wife guaranteed.

"We're having quick-fry steaks," I said. "There's fresh bread, fruit cocktail . . ."

That's as far as I got.

My wife bent me back over the chesterfield and gave me a warm, passionate kiss on the lips. I could feel her undo the bow on my apron.

"Promise you'll respect me in the morning," I whispered.

Jackie stood through dinner!

Jackie stood up for her first meal Saturday and I don't have to tell women what a breakthrough that is.

When my wife broke her leg skiing, she coped with the pain, the plaster cast, and the crutches, but she was unable to eat standing up.

Ordinarily, like other wives and mothers, my wife never sits down through breakfast, lunch, or supper. She's too busy bringing things to the table, cleaning up drinks the kids have spilled, looking for the HP sauce, checking to see what's boiling over on the stove, and clearing away the dirty plates. But that was impossible with her broken leg. She had to sit there through the entire meal, unable to move and wait on the family hand and foot.

It couldn't have been easy. When a digestive system has spent the past nineteen years in a standing position, or at a slow gallop, it isn't simple for it to be plopped down on a chair and forced to handle everything from corn flakes to pickles without the slightest jiggle.

And then there was the problem of the temperature of the food. As a wife and mother of three, Jackie and her esophagus have never had to contend with any food that wasn't room temperature. Ice cream, coffee, mashed potatoes, salad, rolls, any kind of soup, by the time my wife got to them, they were always lukewarm, or lukecold, as the case might be.

You can imagine, then, the strain of not only eating food in an unaccustomed position but also in an unusual condition. Give my wife credit, though, she struggled through her meals without a complaint, and didn't injure herself in any noticeable way. At least, I didn't see a blister form on her lips, or any traces of frostbite.

As Jackie's leg mended, we let her get back to standing part-time through meals, fetching an occasional course, whipping up to get refills of milk, and that sort of thing. But we never asked her to carry really heavy items to the table, and we limited her to fifteen or twenty trips during the course of the meal to the various appliances, the basement, the telephone (the children's friends always call when we're eating), and various other parts of the home.

By bringing her along gently these past weeks, we didn't damage my wife's leg or her stomach and, happily, things are now back to normal.

As I said at the start, Saturday she stood through the entire supper for the first time since her accident. It was a wonderful sight to see her long after the rest of us had finished, standing by the kitchen table with a cup of cold coffee in her hand.

With the care we've given her, there's no reason she shouldn't last for years.

Return to the slopes?

Friends have been bombarding me with the same question in recent weeks: will Jackie make a comeback as a skier?

As you may recall, my wife spent most of last winter as a patient; and I spent most of last winter as an impatient. That's because my wife fell down a mountain and broke her leg, and my heart, in two places. My wife's après-ski outfit consisted of a plaster cast from her hip to her ankle; mine was an apron and a broom.

Undoubtedly it will come as an awful shock to you to learn that I now regard skiing with the same affection I have for boils or a nasty sinus infection. I did not enjoy watching me do dishes, chase kids, and make beds. And the convalescence took so long!

But what could I expect? If it takes a month for my wife to get around to mending my socks, I should have known it would take the better part of a year for her to mend an entire leg.

Fortunately, Jackie is back on her feet – and it's the beginning of a new ski season. Will she once again take to the hills, there to slide on shimmering sheets of snow right into the first-aid shack at the bottom of the cliff?

Over my dead body, I say. I do not intend to spend this winter watching people write funny things on my wife's leg while I try to get supper ready.

However, fate has played me a dirty trick. Not long ago I did a television show with the French champion, Jean Claude Killy. In the course of the evening, I told Killy that my wife had broken her leg last winter in a spill and he was sympathetic. He mentioned that he had suffered two fractures, too, on his way to three gold medals at the Olympics.

"Of course she will ski again," Killy encouraged.

I blushed and said of course. If there's one thing I hate, it's being accused of trying to run my wife's life, especially when I'm trying to run my wife's life. But under my breath I muttered that Jackie would ski again when Pierre Trudeau gives up kissing girls, when Vancouverites develop an inferiority complex, when Toronto Argos win a Grey Cup, when Dalton Camp sends a valentine to Allan MacEachen.

Later in the evening a girl named Penny who works with Killy on his ski shows asked my address. Since she was blonde, young, and gorgeous, I gave it. Of course she had an excuse – "Jean Claude wants it," she explained.

But – shy girl! – I could see through her little game. Obviously she has a hangup for middle-aged, overweight men with receding hairlines and a mole in their nose.

Or so I told myself.

A week later there was a package in the mail addressed to Jackie and inside was an autographed picture from Jean Claude Killy. My wife was delighted. She showed the picture to all her friends and pointed out that it had been inscribed,

"To Jackie," which gave it even extra prestige.

"I hope this doesn't give you any ideas about skiing again this winter," I grumbled.

"Don't be silly," Jackie said. "The thought hasn't entered my mind."

However, on the first snowfall of the year, Jackie looked outside and I distinctly heard her whisper, "Track!" Apparently, she's getting the old bug again.

Well, I've decided to let her — provided she can find where I've buried her skis in the backyard.

My Wife the Artist

Beauty in hair of the dog

All my wife asks of a hobby is three things: 1. It must be more fun than ironing. (My wife considers getting her appendix out more fun than ironing so it's not a very serious restriction.) 2. It must provide an excuse for locking herself in a room alone when Jane, Richard, and Stephen are fighting over what program to watch on TV. 3. And it must be non-fattening.

Her latest hobby meets all the requirements. My wife is now making wall hangings.

Mind you, these aren't your run-of-the-mill wall hangings – a little anchor from a World War II destroyer, two tin cans, and a bunch of fishermen's net.

Oh, no.

These wall hangings are very classy. In fact, they have pedigrees – literally. They're made from dog hair.

Doesn't that sound exciting?

Jackie collects the hair from neighbourhood mutts, spins it into yarn, and then whips out another – ahem – objet d'arf.

Her latest masterpiece, for example, is made from Bippy (a sheepdog), Fleur (a setter), Sarah (a samoyed), and Lassie (a collie). It's a four-woof production that even I must admit is my wife's best to date. With promotion, and a beret, my wife could become another Vincent Van Growl.

Originally, I had a lot of doubts when my wife announced her plans to weave some of our friends' dogs into decorative patterns. If God had intended dogs to be wall hangings, I told her, He would have made them flatter and given them hooks instead of ears. Nobody, I added, wants a wall hanging that chases cats, ha, ha, or drools every time you go near it with your dinner. Besides, where would we get a flea collar big enough for a living-room wall?

My wife paid no attention and, like a blue serge suit, continued to pick up dog hair wherever she could. As a result, we're now the proud possessors of a veritable litter of wall hangings; and they're all housebroken. No matter who calls – the National Gallery or the Sportsman show – Jackie is ready.

By the way, we have a friend who owns a wolf and Jackie is toying with the idea of weaving wolf hair into her next project. It could be a first – a wall hanging that protects itself from art thieves.

Sic 'em, boy!

Super-sniffer foiled in kitchen

I have always had the utmost faith in my nose. In forty-five years of sniffing, it has never let me down as a food detector. The type of food is unimportant – cheese omelettes, bagels, homemade grape jelly, banana cream pie, Winnipeg goldeye, apples. If it's in the house, my nose knows. My wife only has to turn in her recipe book to the page marked Swiss steak and I can tell, with one nostril tied behind my back.

Immodest as it may seem, I believe I have one of the truly great noses of our time. If there were an Olympic event for noses, I'm sure I'd take the gold for Canada.

Yesterday, however, my nose made a mistake. And a dandy. I hadn't gotten out of my coat in the hallway when my nose began to twitch. Then it quivered. Finally it was in full flare.

"You've got something cooking," I announced to my wife.

I then galloped to the kitchen.

"I thought so!" I said joyously, lifting off the top of a pot simmering on the stove. "Noodle – with onions and other goodies. When do we eat?"

"That's not for dinner," my wife chided.

"What do you mean it's not for dinner?" I demanded.

"It's not dinner," came her reply. "It's not even food. It's Sarah."

"Sarah? You mean you've cooked our dog? Well, we'll discuss that later. She certainly smells delicious."

"Don't be silly. I haven't cooked all of Sarah, just her hair."

"Her hair?"

"You know I've been collecting Sarah's hair and making it into yarn," my wife amplified. "Well, I want to dye it, so I'm boiling it with onion skins and a few things."

"You mean that what smells so good on the stove is our dog's hair?"

"Yes."

"What are we having for dinner?" I asked.

"Frozen dinners. I've been too busy dyeing to cook."

"I hate frozen dinners," I muttered. "Couldn't we at least try Sarah's hair? Throw in a few carrots and some potatoes and . . ."

"No."

"But my nose tells me . . ."

"Your nose is wrong," my wife stated. "Besides, I don't want to kiss anyone with Samoyed breath."

I only hope my nose doesn't develop an inferiority complex over the whole affair.

My wife's conscience is spoiling us

For some time my wife has toyed with the idea of going back to school on a regular basis, and this September she did it. Jackie's a freshperson at the Ontario College of Art. Mind you, she attends her course in fibres (weaving and stuff) only one day a week, but already there has been a tremendous change in our lives.

Frankly, things have never been so good at home. The reason, of course, is Jackie's terrific sense of guilt at leaving her little ones (Richard, 10, Jane, 13, Stephen, 15, and Gary, 46) on their own while she attends class. She's determined to prove that her decision will in no way affect the quality of life at home.

As a result, my wife has spent dozens of extra hours over the stove ever since she tiptoed back into the halls of academe. The day before her class, for example, she whips up batches of great muffins and buns so that breakfast on school morning will be nothing to complain about. As well, she stacks up plates of goodies (even smashing desserts) so that the children, when they come home at noon, will be too busy eating to notice the empty place at the sink where, in years past, they've grown accustomed to seeing their mother stand through lunch.

Dinner? Well, that's the best meal of the week now, even topping the Sunday performance. Because Jackie whips in at the last minute, she prepares the previous night and to date we've had favourites of mine like chili, Austrian stews, and lasagna.

Naturally, no guilty person's menu would be complete without fresh-baked pie and ice cream, the final touch in keeping my wife's hangups under control.

It's been absolutely wonderful living with Jackie's conscience. I'll tell you how guilty my wife feels about abandoning us once a week: yesterday, I caught her ironing!

Not only that, in the past week she has cleaned all the downstairs windows and made them so spotless at least four birds have flown into them, stubbing their beaks on the polished glass. If you walked into our front room, you would never believe it was the home of a "part-time" mother, which is just as Jackie wants it.

Already the children are looking through the school brochure in the hope of finding other courses for Mother, something that would vault us into even dizzier heights of posh living.

Considering the richness of the food so far, I personally feel my digestion could take only one more subject, two at the very most. In fact, if Jackie ever becomes a full-time student, my weight could easily soar over the 300-pound mark by the time she graduates.

Guilt! Isn't it wonderful?

School is dangerous for Mother

When my wife decided last September to return to school on a part-time basis, she felt she was ready to face the brave new world. Now Jackie's not so sure.

She didn't mind being the only one in class wearing eye makeup, a bra, and a T-shirt without something suggestive stencilled on the front. But her latest experience in the halls of academe has been truly shattering, even worse than that first time Jackie told a fellow student she had a sixteen-year-old son, and the person wasn't surprised.

What happened was this. My wife was in one of those student haunts last week and was struck by a display of ceramic pipes being offered for sale by a young man. As it happens, we've been looking for a Christmas present for my brother.

(Yes, I know Christmas was weeks ago, but my brother still hasn't sent me my birthday present and my birthday was last November, so I still have loads of time.)

"How much are the pipes?" my wife asked.

"Two dollars, or three joints," he answered.

"Pardon?" was my wife's response.

"Two dollars, or three joints," he repeated.

"Joints?"

"Yes – joints."

To a woman who spends each morning trying to shovel hot porridge into her three children and scraping dog hair off the rug, "joints" is something to do with arthritis.

But at long last a light flashed on.

"Oh, joints – like in marijuana," my wife-turned-student said.

The young man stared across the generation gap, just as puzzled as my wife.

"I'm sorry, I only have cash," Jackie continued, trying desperately to retrieve her cool after the earlier fumble.

"Too bad," he commented.

By now my wife wanted to back out of the transaction, but it was too late. She handed over the money, and he gave her the pipe.

Driving home that evening my wife told me about her experience. "Maybe the guy was just kidding," I suggested. "He saw your ironed jeans, combed hair, and wedding ring and decided to pull your leg."

She said he seemed sincere.

"Where's the pipe?" I asked.

My wife brought out her purchase — a clay pipe about five inches long with a very tiny bowl.

"For heaven's sake, that's a pot pipe," I exclaimed. "You've bought a pipe for dope."

That was the final blow. Jackie was totally deflated.

Now we've got to think of some way to get ride of the pipe before the Mounties come down on our neck, put my wife under a glaring light, and demand to know the name of her "connection."

In the meantime, I've made Jackie promise not to talk to strangers on her way to school again.

Art for art's sake?

Is there no end to the crises around the home? The Ontario College of Art displayed the work of some of its students at an open house recently and among the objets d'art were two bits of weaving by Jackie Lautens.

Yes, the wife.

The one was a wall hanging, orange, blue, and big enough to cover all sorts of nicks in the plaster (which is how we use it); and the other was a butterfly that hangs from the ceiling by threads.

The reason I describe them in such lush detail is because, after the exhibition, the missus was handed the names of nine people who had signed a list to indicate their interest in buying her creations. And they were real names, too — none of this "A. Hitler, Berlin" or "Mao Tse-tung, Scarborough."

There wasn't even a single "I.M. Loony" on the paper.
Of course I was thrilled.

"Well, now the old filthy lucre starts rolling in," I said sensitively, rubbing my hands together in eager anticipation.

"What do you mean?" Jackie asked.

"I mean, after all these years of watching you spin up old dog hair and turn the laundry room into a dyeing works, it's going to be wonderful to get some money in for a change."

"I'm not selling my things," she corrected.

"Are you joking?" I demanded. "Aren't you going to call these people and see how much they're willing to fork over for the butterfly and the wall hanging?"

"Of course not. I worked months on those things and they mean too much to me to sell to strangers. Besides, some of the wool in the butterfly came from our own dog, and there are bits of McVean's Samoyed in the other one."

"This is a chance to make your first sale as an artist," I pointed out.

"No," was her short reply.

"Look, Da Vinci sold his stuff; Michelangelo was always ready to knock off a ceiling for a few bucks; Picasso had no objections to taking a bit in exchange for a scribble or two."

"That's their affair," Jackie sniffed. "I slaved over those things and I don't want to part with them now."

"That's not very professional," I said. "Besides, we could use the money. We've got to buy a house in Toronto and we need every spare $100,000 we can lay our hands on. Who knows, you may become famous."

In an obvious attempt to play on male vanity, my wife responded by asking, "Would you want to be known as Jackie Lautens' husband?"

"Yes, if it paid well enough," I told her.

"I'd sooner sell my children," the artist vowed.

"Well, you're the boss," I surrendered. "How much do you think we could get for them?"

The kick on the shins told me the wife was not amused.

With all the greedy artists in the world, how come I happened to get stuck with one who wants to keep her amateur status?

Moving to Toronto

The grass is greener
now that we've sold

It's amazing how much work you have to do before a house is fit to move out of. Our repairs began only moments after we had closed the deal on our home.

"Before we move, I think you should replace the washers in the bathroom taps," Jackie advised. "I wouldn't want to leave a leaky faucet for the new people." That evening I put in new washers, and strained myself in the groin area.

Next came the fireplace. "If you got some acid you could scrub off the smoke stains on the fireplace stone," my wife suggested. "It would look much better for the new people." I bought the acid, cleaned the fireplace, and hardly got any acid at all on my face, hands, and body.

"This would be a good day to take off the screens and wash the windows," my wife advised the first Saturday morning after our sale. Several screens haven't been off since the day we moved in but I did as I was told, transforming each window into a little jewel.

"I wouldn't want to leave our lawn looking like this," was Jackie's next comment, staring out at a sea of dandelions and other broad-leafed weeds. I picked up a bag of Dr. Garden's Weed No-No and spread it evenly over the front and back yard in a spreader rented from the hardware store. In between time, I glued in a bit of parquet floor which (according to my wife) sounded a little loose.

This past week I got home from work and my wife had a new chore for me. "I'm certain there's a bird or something in our chimney," she advised. "You'd better go up on the roof and look. I don't want anyone to say we left a house with a bird in the chimney."

I climbed the TV tower, jumped to the roof, and peered down the chimney, getting only a little soot on my suit. "I can't see anything," I shouted to Jackie.

"Are you certain?"

"Fairly certain."

"Get a flashlight and look down."

Even a flashlight (yes, I had to climb down from the roof and back up again) showed no sign of an intruder, but my wife asked me to cover the chimney with a protective bit of wiring so no bird or animal will be able to get into the chimney after the new people take over.

Two days ago we reached another milestone. After we started up the swimming pool for the new people, we experienced a minor problem with leakage, nothing I couldn't live with, but my wife wasn't satisfied.

Ian (our pool man) diagnosed the problem as a valve at the bottom of the pool. A frogman spent thirty minutes yesterday at the bottom of our pool making the necessary repairs, and I don't even want to think about what it will cost.

At this moment my wife is scrubbing cupboards, touching up paint, vacuuming drapes, doing masonry repairs, cleaning the built-in stove, for heaven's sake – for the new people.

Our house never looked so good, and now I'm sorry we're leaving.

On reading real-estate ads

After commuting to work (thirty-one miles each way) for

nearly fourteen years, I've decided it's time to move into big, bad Toronto. So we've sold our house (to a nice couple from Calgary) and are going through the real-estate ads each evening.

Even though we're novices, my wife and I are catching on to certain phrases copywriters use in describing property that's for sale. For example, "close to everything" means there's no front lawn and you're so close to the street you'll think the buses are going through your living room.

"Picturesque neighbourhood" – there are winos sprawled over the sidewalk.

"Can be turned into income property" – the place has a basement and enough room behind the furnace to hang a hammock.

"Handyman's special" – there's no ceiling in the bedroom, the wiring has been condemned, and you have to shinny a rope to get upstairs.

"Victorian gem" – if you weigh over 135 pounds you won't fit in the kitchen.

"Can't be duplicated at the price" – no, but it can be for $25,000 less in Hamilton.

"For those who want something better" – it's out of your price range.

"Ravine lot" – step outside the back door and its seventy-five feet straight down.

"Move in for only $5,000 down" – and pay $1,200 a month carrying charges.

"Architect designed" – the place has a bar in the basement made with leftover lumber by a previous tenant who took a shop course at high school.

"Loads of extras" – there's a shower in the bath tub.

"Only minutes from downtown" – by Soyuz rocket, and not during the rush hour.

"Newly decorated" – the living room has been painted within the past ten years, in maroon.

"Lawyer's home" – the place has been lived in for eighteen

months by a motorcycle gang, but the second mortgage on the place is held by a man named Lawyer who lives in Miami year round.

"In prestige area" – it's almost half a block from an all-night pizza parlor.

"Ideal for executive couple" – there's only one bedroom and it's listed at over $100,000.

"Wake up each morning with the birds" – there's a chicken plucker next door.

"Part of Toronto's past" – the house will have to be gutted and rebuilt.

"Move into this centrally located beauty and throw away your car keys" – there's no garage, side drive, or spot on the street for your car.

"Pool-size lot" – unfortunately, you'll have to tear down the house if you want to put a pool on it, however.

"Three or four-bedroom home" – one of the bedrooms has a large closet.

"Gourmet kitchen" – the can opener on the wall goes with the house.

Yes, we're getting the swing of it.

We leave for an exotic foreign post

As long as I can remember I've tried to talk my employer(s) into letting me take my column to some foreign city for a year or two. Oh, to be bedded down in Chelsea, nipping up to the palace ever now and then to give the Queen a bit of advice; or to be meeting some contact in the sewers of Copenhagen, exchanging passwords and microfilm behind the upturned collars of our trenchcoats.

Lovely!

Alas! The farthest I ever got was the apartments-for-rent column of the Paris edition of the *Herald-Tribune*. That was in 1973, and then that little plan was scrapped, too. It seemed fate never intended me to be another Joe Schlesinger, or an Ernest-what's-his-name.

However, at long last my boyhood dream has come true. Even as you read this I am on my way to an exciting assignment in a strange and mysterious place. Yes, today we are moving into Toronto.

Some of you may not think that's quite like London, Moscow, Vienna, Rome, or the previously mentioned Paris, but when you were born in Fort William and have lived most of your life in the Hamilton (Ont.) area, Toronto is a foreign assignment.

In fact, my Hamilton friends feel we're nuts to give up a 220-foot frontage in the suburbs (Burlington) to move into Toronto, and are certain they'll never see us again. Not alive. When we say we've bought a house in DOWNTOWN Toronto, and the house is only fourteen feet wide, they bite their lips, and rush home to sew black bands on the arms of their shirts or dresses.

But I feel it's time to explore a new culture, to study the customs of a different society. Do the people in Toronto really eat their young, as street gossips in Hamilton say? Is it true they breathe air without steel filings and chunks of cinder in it? Gosh, is it possible they don't take off their hats and place them over their chests when any member of the Tiger-Cats walks by?

Well, we'll find out.

Of course, I've told the children not to laugh when they see people in the street without safety shoes, hardhats, and a number scratched on the side of a lunch-pail with a nail. I've also instructed them to avoid the drinking water for the first while, to look at a picture of a tree whenever they feel home sick, and not to play with any neighbourhood children who get more than $100 a week allowance from their parents.

I don't want them snickering either when somebody tries to tell them they have trains in Toronto that run under the ground. When you're from out-of-town, people in Toronto will tell you anything.

In any case, tonight we'll be in our new beds (the old ones had to be sold because they wouldn't fit) and in our new home, wondering what adventures will befall us in the days ahead.

At the end of the week we plan to go down to Lake Ontario and throw bottles with messages in them to our friends in Hamilton. We want them to know we've at least got this far safely.

Jackie's taut nerves a moving story

Believe me, it was our plan to move into Toronto quietly. And, except for the three visits by police, several shouting matches, a traffic jam you wouldn't believe, an angry march by the residents' association, one near fistfight, and the car that had to be towed away, it went like clockwork.

In fact, it may be the best move we've ever made. I'm sure my wife will agree, once I coax her down from the drapes.

Jackie says she never wants to show her face in public again, but then she always says that after she's been the central figure in a mob scene or riot.

For heaven's sake, the movers did arrive right on time, they didn't break anything, and Jerry (the husky mover) didn't actually land any punches during the worst of it. Surely that's worth something.

Yes, it was unfortunate that a tourist's car was parked illegally in front of our new address when the movers arrived. And, yes, it did make things awkward when the moving van cut off all traffic because it couldn't be parked next to the curb (because of the illegally parked car). And I guess the motorists who jammed the street in the middle of the morning rush hour did say some nasty things, and may even have landed a couple of vicious kicks on the van's tires.

But nobody had to go to hospital after the mêlée, and Jerry (the mover) did seem to settle things down when he stood in the middle of the pavement and challenged anyone who didn't like the way the van was parked (in the middle of the road) to do something about it. When the police arrived (for the first time) they agreed Jerry was only doing his job, and didn't make a single arrest or fingerprint anyone.

Mind you, I wish the cars hadn't tried to squeeze past by going up over the curb and brushing into the lilac trees the residents' association prizes so much. Especially the big bus. If that hadn't happened, maybe our new neighbours wouldn't have come out in force, threatened the motorists, taken down licence numbers, and called police a second time.

At least Jerry and Harold (the other mover) weren't involved in that and, when they were asked whose stuff they were moving, they didn't give our name. Jerry assured us of that. Besides, I don't think the person who came with the pad and jotted down notes was a newspaper reporter, as Jackie feared. He probably was only a member of the residents' association, or a plainclothesman.

Certainly conditions improved and there was hardly any

honking or obscene gestures after the police came the third time and towed away the illegally parked car that was the start of the trouble anyway.

The entire fuss couldn't have lasted more than six hours, and I'd bet nobody would recognize my wife since she spent most of the moving morning hiding in the closet. So there's no reason for her to be afraid to come out now that the police, tow trucks, movers, the thirty or forty angry motorists, etc. have gone.

Heck, a cold cloth on her forehead, a couple of Aspirin, and six weeks' total rest, and she'll be right as rain again. Or just about.

Big city life opened my eyes

Doesn't take long, does it? To lose the old winsome, small-town charm, I mean. We've only been in Toronto a couple of days as full-time residents and I can already see the change in me.

Sweet I was when we arrived. Saccharin wouldn't melt in my mouth and I wouldn't know a double entendre if I tripped over it (them?). Just a country lad with my worldly goods in an A & P shopping bag (including my Lawrence Welk record collection), a spear of grass hanging from my lips, and wide-eyed enough you could drive a truck up the bridge of my nose. But that's all over now and I have become sophisticated.

The transformation took place last evening in a small restaurant not far from our new home, a place where (so I was told) they make terrific hamburgs and Coke floats. In we walked, the missus and myself, and after a bit, the hostess took us to an empty table where we had a chance to look over the list of eats.

"I hate to say anything," I whispered to my wife, "but did you notice anything unusual about the hostess?"

My wife said she didn't.

I took her word and dropped the subject until we were halfway through our hamburgs.

"Psst," I murmured. "Take another look at the hostess."

"What am I supposed to be looking for?" the wife answered.

"I don't think she's wearing anything under her T-shirt," I said. "She hasn't got a B-R-A."

"Are you just catching on to that?" was the curt reply. "Boy, are you slow."

Well, that may have been the point when I realized I was really in The Big City because, in the sticks, you don't get hamburgs with that kind of works. Just days ago (when I was still a Hamiltonian, and nice) I'd have blushed at any young thing who showed me to my seat in a restaurant in that condition.

Not now.

I carefully took my eyeglasses out of my pocket and pretended to polish them while, in actual fact, I was staring at her reflection in my lenses. Yes, I must have ogled my spectacles at least a half-dozen times.

Bold as brass, if you please. Once I caught a glimpse in the mirror across the room, and another time I picked up my knife and saw her full frontal while she cleared off a table. Pure debauchery, it was, and still daylight, too.

Of course, I was shocked to think I'd fallen this far down the path of sin since my Trail Ranger days at First United Church in Hamilton, and that I'll probably have to wear a scarlet "S" on my forehead when they hear back home how I've been carrying on. But that's the way it happens. One day hearts and flowers, and the next (wink, wink) you're a sport with a reputation to live down.

Still, when in Toronto you have to do what the Torontonians do and, if that's how they serve hamburgs, well, what's a body to do?

Golly, I never saw a Big Mac with fixin's like that.

Commuting drove me to the city

As I write this I've been a resident of Toronto exactly 548 hours and thirty-two minutes. How can I be so precise? Because I drove into the yard behind our new home 548 hours and thirty-two minutes ago, and the car hasn't moved since. When you've been commuting as long as I have (fourteen years) you take note of such facts in your life.

The previous record for my car being idle was just under thirty-two minutes, a mark set in 1967 on a day when I had my appendix out, and Jane didn't have to go to her dance lessons. Ordinarily I spent a minimum of an hour and a half each day behind the wheel, staring up the tailpipe of a semi hauling concrete blocks, or musing over whether the Buick in back would notice traffic had stopped before it wound up in my front seat.

So I can't believe it's 548 hours and thirty-two, I mean thirty-six minutes since I said naughty things under my breath about a bus driver cutting into my lane, or heard the latest traffic report from some radio station's helicopter and wanted to eat the upholstery in my car.

I haven't pumped gas, chauffeured kids, begged a parking-lot attendant to let me in at $3.50 per beg, been caught in the middle of a drag race between a souped-up Harley and a panel truck with "Don't laugh – your daughter may be inside" painted on the fenders. For heaven's sake, I haven't even thrown on my brakes at the last second to avoid hitting a truck filled with melons (doing 25 mph in a 60 zone) and thrown my entire family headfirst into the windshield.

Ho, ho, ho!

My sunglasses are still in the car and, as a matter of princi-ple, I've even refused to open the car door for them.

When we decided to move, I made only one stipulation: that the house, apartment, cave, cardboard carton, etc., would have to be within walking distance of work. Well, I'm two miles from the office, and I trudge it every day with a song in my heart, looking at shop windows and girls (not necessarily in that order), and not at the gas gauge and somebody's off-colour bumper sticker.

Of course it won't last. Perhaps some day I'll have to get the car out again (when Jane gets married, for example, or when I'm invited to take part in the city of Hamilton's bicentennial celebrations in 2046 A.D.).

Believe me, I have nothing personal against my car; it's been dependable, loyal, and an absolute brick through every kind of traffic jam, February blizzard, and Highway 10 slow-down. But it's time we both had a rest.

So if you see a pedestrian during rush hour standing by the ramp to the expressway (the one with traffic backed up to Oshawa), and he's cackling and jumping up and down, and rubbing his hands together, don't offer him a ride.

He's been on one for fourteen years.

Houses cost enough to make you . . . grin

The last thing a person wants to know is how much the previous owner paid for your house, especially if he bought it ten years ago. However, try as you might, the subject invariably seems to pop up in conversation.

A few days ago I met an old college pal of mine named Sam, and Sam was with another lawyer named Monty. After we were introduced, Monty said: "I see you've just moved to Toronto."

I told him he was correct.

"Where did you buy?" was his next question.

I gave him the location.

"Great location," Monty conceded, "near everything. What did you pay?"

Before I realized what I was doing, I revealed the figure.

Monty said he could have guessed it. "That's about what property is going for now in that area."

Then came the zinger.

"Do you know what you could have picked that house up for a few years ago?" Monty wanted to know.

I pretended not to hear and made some comment about the weather, or El Salvador, or our balance of trade problems with the United States. I can't remember exactly which.

"How long did the previous owner live in the house?" Monty persisted.

I could think of no way out short of cardiac arrest, so I told him.

"I'd say he got it then for $12,000, $15,000 tops."

I could feel the blood draining even from my hair because (as you may have guessed) we paid a teensy weensy bit more for the house than that. Of course it's been renovated and . . . but $15,000!

As soon as I got home I blurted the details to my wife. "Do you know what a lawyer said we could have bought this house for ten years ago?"

My wife said she didn't want to know.

"Guess," I insisted.

She refused to hazard a price and walked into the kitchen. "Dinner's in ten minutes," was her only comment.

"$15,000," I announced. "Maybe $12,000."

My wife (whose name is on half the mortgage) moaned something almost inaudible and put her head between her knees.

All through the evening the two of us were quiet, mulling over my conversation with Monty.

"If I don't miss a day's work, and get some outside jobs, I'll have the house paid for by 2006 A.D.," I finally said in an attempt to cheer her up. "I'll only be seventy-seven."

The comment had no noticeable effect on my wife's mood. However, as we were getting into bed, the faintest trace of a smile crept across Jackie's face.

"Why the grin?" I asked.

"I was just thinking what we paid for our old house in 1966, and what we sold it for," she replied.

Undoubtedly Monty already knows.

Every man for himself in ladies' shoe department

Life in the inner city is not all ice cream and coloured balloons. There are dark moments, too, and the missus had one just yesterday. There was a shoe sale on at our corner department store and, never one to turn her back on saving a buck, Jackie rushed right over with her size nine feet. Both of them.

She was fingering through the bin of Tender Tootsies when she found exactly what she wanted: a pair of blue suede jobs that would be just dreamy with the new slacks. Not flashy, the right height heel, serviceable enough to wear to the office, but also the kind of thing that could be worn when hubby takes her out for the champagne dinner and a wild night of dancing at some smart night spot.

("Hubby" doesn't actually take her out for champagne dinners, etc.; I put that bit in to make me look good.)

Anyway, Mrs. Lautens slipped on the blue suede jobs, moved the little piggies around, and asked the clerk if she had a half-size larger. They were just a little tight. The salesperson checked and said, yes, there was one pair of shoes in that style, size 9½, but they were being tried on at that very moment by another customer. And the clerk pointed out a young man in his mid-twenties slipping into the footwear Jackie wanted.

Of course my wife was taken aback. Over the years she has had some monumental struggles over remnant counters, in the lingerie section, on either side of the blouse rack, and so on. But, up to this point, Jackie's adversary for the bargains has always been another woman: a teen-ager with arms sturdy enough to shred a tractor; a society matron with a pearl brooch on her chest but pure killer in her heart; a suburban housewife with enough megawatts in her smile to melt stone,

175

and elbows that stun with a single blow; an office worker who, with feet in position, stands her ground like the TD Centre. But always a woman.

Under normal circumstances Jackie might merely have snatched the shoes she wanted from her competitor's hand, and put in the knee if there were any serious protest. That *modus operandi* has stood her in good stead in all her years as a bargain-hunter. But against a man? It seemed, well, unfeminine.

Jackie watched him try on both shoes, walk up and down the carpet, look into the floor mirror, and do little turns to check for heel slippage. They were agonizing moments.

Every instinct was for upending the rival and stripping his feet of the shoes she wanted, breaking them off (the feet, I mean) at the ankle if there was no other way. However, my wife waited, keeping her cool, and not making even a single devastating comment like "They don't go with your eyes."

Finally, he made his decision: he wanted the blue suede shoes. Jackie was heartbroken over the loss, so heartbroken she didn't even bother to look for other shoes.

Out of this nasty little incident has come something positive, however. In the future, if Jackie comes up against a man shopping for himself in the women's section of any of her favourite stores, she vows there'll be no more special treatment, especially if he reaches for the $19.95 drastically reduced item she has her eye on. As far as my wife is concerned, it's no more nice gal.

Parting Shots

A mother-in-law story

I don't do mother-in-law material. And that's not because I have a father-in-law (Ted) who is an ex-football player, wrestler, and weightlifter, a man who finds it amusing to lift up chesterfields while somebody is innocently sleeping in same.

No, the reasons I don't do mother-in-law material are because: (1) I find mother-in-law jokes coarse and sexist; (2) mother-in-law slams are a cheap way to get laughs; (3) I don't enjoy sleeping in the small back bedroom, the one with the bad pillows, by myself.

However, I have to break a twenty-five-year rule today to relate the latest episode involving Irene, the Resident Love Goddess's mother and queen of the shopping plazas. (Shopping plazas are to Irene what deficits are to Marc Lalonde. She will go anywhere, provided you pass a mall with a feature on anything.)

Anyway, a few days ago I was with my in-laws when wife Jackie asked her mother whatever had happened to a painting she remembered hanging on the family front room wall, a picture with special meaning to her. The painting was of a ski hill at St. Sauveur in the Laurentians and was done by Paul Duff, a family friend, when Duff was fifteen or sixteen.

I should explain Duff has a pretty good reputation now as a Canadian artist. He grew up in the Hamilton area and went to McMaster University (where I met him). After graduation he continued in art, winding up for many years in South America, in Rio. Not long ago he had a major exhibition in Toronto at one of those smart little galleries near Hazelton Lanes and his pictures are now worth a thousand or two.

To get back to the story, Jackie asked about this early Duff picture that held so many childhood memories for her. Jackie as a tot attended a bunny school run by Paul Duff's mother, which explains why the piece of real art came into my in-laws' possession.

Irene said she still had the oil but it was now in a closet. Would Jackie like to see it?

Of course Jackie would.

Irene went to fetch the picture as the years rolled back in my wife's mind and visions of the current worth of the picture danced in her head. How many Duff originals of that period could be around?

Irene came back into the room and unveiled the Duff. To some silence. "It looks, well, it looks different," Jackie at last mentioned to her mother.

"It's the same picture," my mother-in-law assured, holding up the item in question, a painting about the size of a TV screen.

"Are you sure?" Jackie asked.

"Yes," Irene affirmed. "A few years ago the snow on the hill started to look a little yellow so I painted it over. Other than that, it's the same."

"You painted over the picture?" my wife asked in some shock.

"Yes. It's much whiter now, and the shadows are gone, too."

Well, as I explained to a shaken Jackie later, we can at least be thankful my mother-in-law used a brush, not a roller.

Unspoiled resorts for birds

Some people just don't know when to stop when they're rolling with a really good story.

Take these friends of ours who have just come back from a holiday. They dropped over the other evening to show off their fabulous tans and two albums of snapshots, and they were getting a lot of encouraging envy, especially from my wife when they described how warm this place they visited was. Their descriptions of the fresh fish dinners, the clear water, and the long stretches of sand were also extremely impressive. In fact, Jackie – who is so desperate for a holiday right now she'd sign on with a Russian trawler as a deckhand – was almost drooling.

However, our friends went one step too far.

"You should go there while it's still unspoiled," the husband recommended.

That did it.

"Unspoiled?"

For heaven's sake, what my wife is looking for in a holiday is a place that is spoiled, and spoiled a heck of a lot. In her opinion, it's almost impossible to spoil a place too much. Not for her the remote outpost where you can climb a coconut tree for lunch, sleep on a bare surplus cot under the stars, and pick exotic insects out of your travel brochures. No, even having a rare blue snake slither out of your sleeping bag holds no charm for Mrs. Lautens. Call her a spoilsport if you want, but that is the fact of the matter.

What Jackie likes on a holiday is room service. She likes good plumbing, showers in the actual room, sturdy window screens, a nice pool (heated), a place to plug in a razor in case the legs get a little fuzzy, an elevator if there are more than two storeys to the building, parking arrangements, a front desk where you can pick up mail from home.

Bed linen? Well, you can change it twice a day if you like and Jackie will never complain. There is no yearning in her to go beddy-byes beside a spiky bush that every bug and his brother probably calls home. She can also do without a wade in the surging virgin ocean, the one in which she is always certain something made of jelly is wrapping around her legs.

No, give the girl a good sidewalk that leads to a shopping plaza, a place where you can get beach towels cheap, an air-conditioned drug store with a forty-four-cent pantyhose special. Throw in a hamburger joint where she can send the kids if she doesn't feel like making dinner and Mrs. Lautens is practically in heaven. That's how spoiled she likes her holiday place to be.

A fireplace with logs already cut and stacked, a comforting door with double lock – and preferably a chain – colour TV in case it rains some night and you can't get out, little packets of shampoo left by the management, towels with enough nap to choke a horse. Oh, yes, and a balcony so you can see all the nature you want, and then pull the drapes when you've had enough.

Now that's what my wife calls a holiday.

You can have those pitch-black nights, the call across the empty land of some creature probably with foot-length teeth, the unexplained paw prints on the hood of the car when you wake up in the morning, the thermostat-less tent.

Give Jackie the spoiled vacation spot every time. Me too.

'57 outfits back in style

You'd think after twenty-two years of marriage Mrs. Lautens would have run out of ways to surprise her veteran husband, but such is not the case. Hardly a day slips by without my eyebrows arching at something the Resident Love Goddess says or does.

Take this past weekend. We were getting ready to go to a dinner party when Jackie appeared in the bedroom, gave a twirl, and asked for an honest opinion of her outfit. That's when I went back on my heels.

No, there were no bits of Jackie showing that shouldn't have, nor was she wearing a King Tut T-shirt with suggestive hieroglyphics on the front. It was more mind-boggling than that. What Jackie was wearing was a two-piece navy suit with padded shoulders and a straight skirt. Not just any old two-piece navy suit. Her going-away suit when we got married!

If memory serves correctly, I first saw the item in the afternoon of April 6, 1957, sometime between saying "I do" and fishing the drinking uncle out of the festive punch bowl. The actual wedding gown has long since been dismembered, cut up (the lace overskirt at least) to serve as fish nets for children wading in a creek behind our old house.

But the going-away suit? I thought it had been sent off long ago to a rummage sale to provide funds for some good work, or that it had provided Christmas supper for a family of needy moths. What a surprise!

"The style is back so I dug it out of the basement closet today," Jackie announced. "Is it okay?"

I said it was swell, figuring swell is the kind of word that should be used to describe a suit that first saw the light of day during the Louis St. Laurent administration.

"I paid $110 for the suit," Mrs. Lautens recalls. "It would be $400 today."

With that last nugget of information I enthused even more, stating the skirt length was perfect by today's standards and that what was in it was obviously the same size as when it belonged to an eighteen-year-old bride. Bum-de-bum-bum.

"One thing you have to promise," Mrs. Lautens said.

"What's that?" I asked.

"Don't go around telling everyone at the party this is my going-away outfit from our wedding. I don't want them to know."

"Why would I do that?"

"Because you're rotten at keeping secrets. I know you."

I promised I wouldn't make a peep.

We arrived at the party and sat down in the front room. I never said a word, not for the longest time. Finally it started to bug me. I knew the joke but nobody else did. I could take it no longer.

"How do you like Jackie's suit?" I asked the other guests. Mrs. Lautens stared at me.

Everyone agreed it was a very smart suit and then I said, "Jackie, tell them the story behind it."

With everyone clamouring for details, Jackie had no choice but to spill all – and got quite a laugh.

On the way home Mrs. Lautens said, "I thought you promised not to tell about my suit."

"I didn't for almost eight minutes," I said. "That's a record for me. But, if you're mad, I promise I won't write about it."

That seemed to satisfy her.

Slipping a surprise into the day

Your veteran observer isn't often shocked. When Ed Broadbent attacks Pierre Trudeau, I don't need a cool cloth for my forehead. When the Leafs lose another, the colour doesn't drain from my cheeks. When taxes go up, the Irish fight, Ronald Reagan and Chairman Andropov issue a pessimistic bulletin, our Margaret writes another sizzling chapter, René Lévesque makes a threat in two languages, or Nick falls off a dock in the latest episode of "The Beachcombers," I don't beg the kindly editor to bestow a humanitarian kiss of life.

I am fairly cool.

However, when it comes to the Resident Love Goddess (RLG), I am always walking around with arched eyebrows and a slight tic in my eye. That's because I never know what to expect next; it's a surprise every day which, when you consider we've been married two months short of twenty-five years, works out to be approximately 9,065 surprises in our relationship.

Take this morning. I was quietly eating my crunchy granola when Jackie walked into the kitchen wearing a half slip. Oh, she had on other things, saucy thought, but she had the half slip over her black skirt.

My first thought was I had missed a fashion, that the "in" way to wear a slip now is over rather than under street clothes. From what I've seen in your favourite daily's fashion section, that wouldn't be all that bizarre; after all, long socks over pants are a rage, too.

Next I wondered if Jackie had decided to shake up the profs at the theology U. where she works three days a week. A flash of slip in the vestibule might just cause a professor of Old Testament Greek to walk into a cement pillar, an amusing prank the RLG is not above.

Third, I pondered the possibility of Jackie finally cracking under the enormous strain of trying to figure out our daughter Jane's love life.

Happily, Mrs. Lautens responded quickly to my puzzled looks and question. "Why do you think I'm wearing a half slip over my skirt?" she said in amazement at my slow thought processes. "To keep off the dog hair, of course."

Perhaps I should back up a paragraph or two. A few days ago our Sarah the Semi-Wonder Dog was minding her own business (our version) when a young dog attacked her and bit her on the shoulder. The details aren't important except to say Sarah has been to the vet's twice for shots, bandages, and the like, and since then has become a regular sap.

Naturally, we've been gushing all sorts of sympathy on the dog, telling her how brave she is to go to the doctor, holding her paw, feeding her tasty biscuit treats. And Sarah has taken to all this "poor baby" stuff like a duck to orange dressing, so to speak, and now hangs around as if stapled to our knees. One of her little tricks, in fact, is to wait until we're seated at the kitchen table for dinner and then plop her head in our laps.

Ordinarily, such behaviour isn't allowed. If we don't put our heads in her lap when she's eating, we don't expect etc. etc. However, with her injury and all, we've been pretty lax with discipline.

So now you know why Jackie wears a slip over her black skirt around the house.

Why didn't I catch on right away?

Intruders beware of Jackie's right hook

The one thing a man needs in this world is the love of a good woman. And if that good woman also packs a punch that can stun a horse, so much the better.

You are looking at a person with the above blessings. Not only can my life mate hug and kiss, she has the kind of biceps you can count on in adversity.

Let me expand. Wednesday evening around nine there was some banging on our front door followed by door-knob rattling. Mrs. Lautens (who was the only one downstairs)

thought it was one of our youngest son's friends acting a little silly, not all that unusual at seventeen.

So she opened the door.

There, staring her in the face, was a total stranger – six feet tall, twenty to twenty-five, and glassy-eyed. He immediately tried to push past Jackie into the house.

Poor simple lad. He didn't know he was dealing with a Hamilton Beach girl. Jackie pushed back. Hard. In fact, she shoved him back onto the porch, almost down the front steps. And then she slammed the door.

"Gary," the Resident Love Goddess shouted. "Some nut's trying to get into the house."

I rushed down the stairs followed by the two strapping sons who had been doing essays in their bedrooms.

Of course by the time I got to the scene, everything was in order. It always is. The would-be intruder was on the front walk, obviously stunned and shocked by the rude welcome he had received. Jackie opened the front door again and called in the dog. Yes, Sarah the Semi-Wonder Dog was on the front porch during the incident and hadn't curled so much as a lip.

I telephoned 911 and within five minutes two cruisers were on the scene and four large policemen piled out. They grabbed the unwelcome visitor who, by this time, had wandered down a neighbour's side alley.

"The guy is on booze and drugs," one of the constables explained to me. "Did he get inside the house?"

"One foot inside," I explained. "Then my wife threw him out."

Within ten minutes the nasty business was over, the glassy-eyed stranger on his way to police headquarters or a detoxification centre.

After things calmed down I mentioned to Jackie that she should be more careful when throwing people out of the house. "Somebody could get hurt," I cautioned.

"If anybody tries to break into my house, that's the chance they take," she replied with fire.

"I don't mean him; I mean you."

"That didn't even enter my mind," Jackie responded, totally calm and unruffled.

It's wonderful having a strong woman around the house.

Sneaking a little on the side

A pair of parents can get into no end of mischief when left unsupervised by their children. Without an inhibiting youthful gaze to keep them in line, well, it's just one madcap moment after another for mommy and daddy.

This summer our Stephen is working in Ottawa, Richard is with his grandparents in the Laurentians, and Jane is on strange shifts as a lifeguard at a city pool. So there you have the perfect setting for all kinds of hijinks, wink, wink.

Take the other evening. I got home at the usual time and the Resident Love Goddess greeted me with the announcement she was going to do something at dinner she had been waiting eighteen years to do.

"What?" I asked, trembling with the kind of excitement only a parent in a child-free home could understand.

"I'm going to put tomatoes in the salad tonight," Jackie said.

I should explain our children absolutely refuse to eat tomatoes and ever since they were old enough to overturn a bowl, we haven't had tomatoes in our salad, except when we go out.

"Not only am I going to cut up a tomato, I'm going to put the slices right on top where they can be seen," she added. Her

eyes smouldered as the wanton words filled the room.

"Do you think we should?" I asked. "What would the kids say if, the first time they leave us alone, we put tomatoes in our salad?"

"They never have to know," was the response.

We sat down and ate our tomato-laced salads, relaxed in the knowledge we wouldn't be disturbed. There is nothing like tomatus uninterruptus. After dinner, we sat in the kitchen, just the two of us, no prying eyes, no admonishing fingers, no restraining "tut, tuts."

"That was fantastic," I said after the salad things were cleared. "Heh, heh, heh, while the kids are away, the parents will play."

"The evening isn't over yet, big boy," were Mrs. Lautens' next words.

"What do you mean?"

"We're going to see 'The Boy Friend.' I've reserved two tickets."

"But it's the middle of the week," I said. "We never go to the show in the middle of the week, not without asking permission."

Jackie sidled up pretty close. "Relax," she said, "and trust me."

Guilt filled every fibre, but I agreed to go, and we sat through "The Boy Friend" just as bold as brass, especially enjoying again "It's Never Too Late To Fall In Love."

When we were courting (in the winter of 1956-57) we saw the show and that became "our" song because I was twenty-eight at the time, Jackie eighteen, and I especially liked the line, "the modern painters of today may paint their pictures faster, but when it comes to skill, I say, you can't beat an old master."

We were walkng home at eleven o'clock, humming "The Boy Friend" songs, the taste of tomatoes from the salad still in our mouths.

"Did the earth move for you tonight?" I asked.

"Yes," Jackie said.

"I just hope some spoilsport does not start a summer campaign with the slogan, 'Kids, do YOU know where your parents are tonight?'" I said. "If we play our cards right, this could be our wildest summer ever."

"Have half a stick of Dentyne, big fella," said the other parent on the loose.

I like family life

Almost every day another "expert" comes along to forecast the end of family life. Thanks to the Pill and new morality and science and take-out chicken, women will soon be free at last. They'll be able to order test-tube babies – and then farm them out to state nurseries.

No need for marriage licences and a rose-covered cottage. The only pitter-patter around the house will come from the shopping computer when it's on the blink.

Instead of making peanut butter sandwiches, women will be able to fulfil themselves. They'll have jobs and dress in Pucci originals and have dozens of boyfriends and learn to play the cello. Life will be a perpetual Saturday night date.

And men? Everybody knows a man isn't a domestic animal. He wants to chase girls and stay out late and keep his pay cheque to himself.

At least that's how these social seers see things.

Well, let me polish that crystal ball again.

Here's one guy who isn't waiting to be "free." They can

peddle their swinging Shangri-la somewhere else. I like being married. I like family life. I like it when I get home at night and the kids shout, "Dad!" and trip over my feet and hug me and smell sweaty because they've been playing all day. That's love, brother.

You can have your parties and fancy clothes and white broadloomed pads and imported sports cars. I'll take those kids.

Sure, Stephen's teeth stick out a bit and Jane's hair is straight and Richard bounces on beds and they all holler and throw punches when I'm trying to nap.

Maybe a test tube and a battalion of technicians could turn out a more efficient product – a true "superbaby." But those kids are part of me and I'm part of them. We share the same heartbeat. They are the result of love, not a mathematical formula whipped up in a government lab. They are what it's all about.

There's one more thing I like about these kids – their mother. I like sitting across the breakfast table from her every morning. I like the way she laughs. I like the way she talks. I like the way she kisses. Besides, I need her and I think she needs me.

It is never boring.

There is no other hand I want to hold.

Separate vacations or a free squeeze at the office party or a key to Hugh Hefner's pool or even an hour to myself every evening don't tempt me. I like it at home. I like to have the kids around raising hell. I like my wife to tell me what happened that day.

Home is cosy and where I want to be. So those prophets of 1984 can get lost. You are looking at a contented man.